# HOW TO DRAW ANIME FOR BEGINNERS STEP BY STEP: MANGA AND ANIME DRAWING TUTORIALS BOOK 1

Sophia Williams

# HOW TO USE A BOOK

THIS BOOK PROVIDES SIMPLE, STEP-BY-STEP INSTRUCTIONS FOR DRAWING ANIME. MUCH ATTENTION IS PAID TO THE FACE AND EYES OF THE CHARACTERS, AS THIS IS THE MOST DIFFICULT FOR MOST NOVICE ANIME ARTISTS.
YOU NEED ONLY A SHEET OF PAPER AND A REGULAR PENCIL. READ THE INSTRUCTIONS AND REPEAT ALL THE STEPS IN THE ILLUSTRATIONS.

# TIPS FOR BEGINNERS:

1. THE PROPORTIONS OF THE BODY. IN THE ANIME, THE BODY OF THE CHARACTERS IS BUILT SO THAT IT SOMEHOW REFLECTS THEIR MOOD. IMPROVE YOUR SKILLS, AND THIS WILL GIVE YOU THE OPPORTUNITY TO CREATE COMPLETELY DIFFERENT PROPORTIONS. AS A RESULT, YOU MAY FIND YOUR OWN STYLE. LOOK AT ANY ANIME COMIC, AND YOU WILL SEE HOW THE SHAPE OF THE BODY CHANGES, EVEN FOR THE SAME HERO.
2. FROM SKETCH TO DETAIL. ALWAYS START WITH A SKETCH AND ONLY THEN GRADUALLY FILL THE DRAWING WITH DETAILS. IF YOU START TO DRAW COMPLEX GLARE ON YOUR EYES, WITHOUT EVEN FINISHING DRAWING YOUR FACE, IT MAY END UP SO THAT THE EYE ISN`T AT ALL WHERE IT IS NEEDED, AND YOU WILL HAVE TO ERASE EVERYTHING. NEVER LEAVE THE NOTICED ERRORS UNATTENDED, EVEN IF THEIR CORRECTION WILL REQUIRE A LOT OF TIME, OR EVEN IF EVERYTHING HAS TO BE STARTED ANEW! GUIDELINES AND SKETCHES HELP YOU ACHIEVE THE BEST AND MOST ACCURATE RESULT.
3. DISTINCTIVE FEATURES OF HEROES. IT CAN HAPPEN TO EVERY COMIC BOOK ARTIST THAT READERS LOSE INTEREST IN HIS WORK. AND ALL BECAUSE THEY FIND ALL THE CHARACTERS TOO SIMILAR. EACH CHARACTER SHOULD HAVE ITS OWN DISTINCTIVE FEATURES, FOR EXAMPLE, IN HAIR, EYES, GROWTH, OR STYLE OF CLOTHING (UNLESS, ACCORDING TO THE AUTHOR'S IDEA, EVERYTHING SHOULD BE THE OTHER WAY AROUND). THINK IN ADVANCE WHAT COLORS, HAIRSTYLES, AND ACCESSORIES WILL SUIT THIS OR THAT HERO. ALSO, YOU CAN BEAT THE PICTURE BY ADDING AN INTERESTING BACKGROUND, THE ELEMENTS SURROUNDING THE HERO, OR THE STORYLINE.
4. FOCUS ON A MIRROR. PUT A SMALL MIRROR IN FRONT OF YOUR PICTURE. THIS IS A GREAT WAY TO IDENTIFY YOUR MISTAKES. YOU WILL NOTICE THAT A SKETCH THAT SEEMED PERFECT TO YOU ACTUALLY HAS FLAWS, SUCH AS, FOR EXAMPLE, CROOKED EYES OR OTHER ANATOMICAL ERRORS. CONTINUE TO WORK ON THE IMAGE UNTIL YOU ARE COMPLETELY SATISFIED WITH THE RESULT.
5. THE FEMALE BODY. THE LINES OF THE FEMALE BODY IN THE ANIME ARE USUALLY VERY SMOOTH AND REFLECT THE IDEAL OF FEMALE BEAUTY IN JAPAN. PRONOUNCED MUSCLES OR AMAZON GIRLS ARE LESS ATTRACTIVE, AND THEREFORE LESS COMMON. HOWEVER, THE TECHNIQUE OF ADDING MAGNIFICENT BREASTS TO DISTINGUISH AN ADULT GIRL FROM A GIRL IS VERY COMMON.

# CONTENT

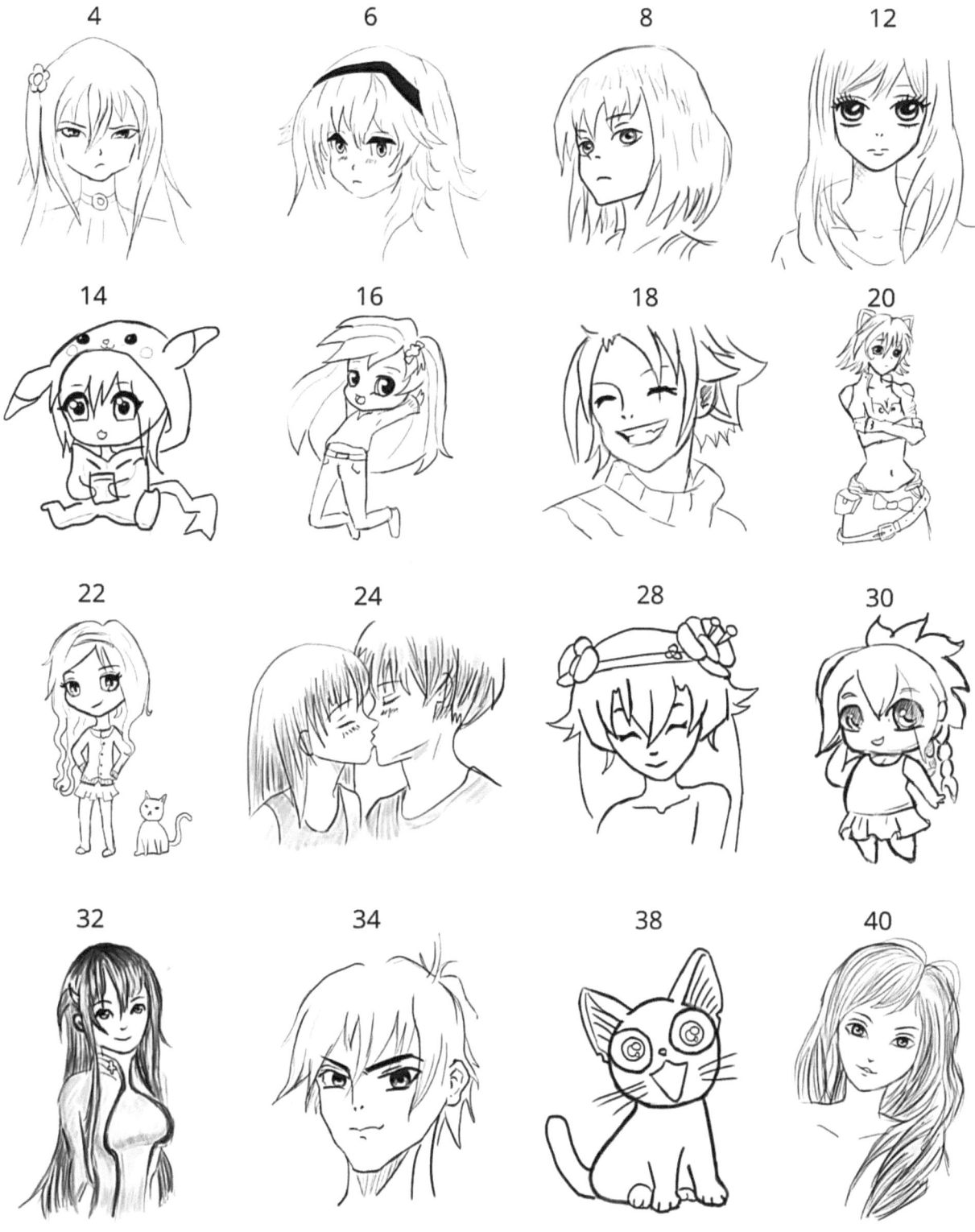

1. DRAW A CIRCLE. THIS IS THE FOUNDATION OF THE FACE. DIVIDE THE CIRCLE INTO TWO EQUAL PARTS AND DRAW EYES AND EYEBROWS.

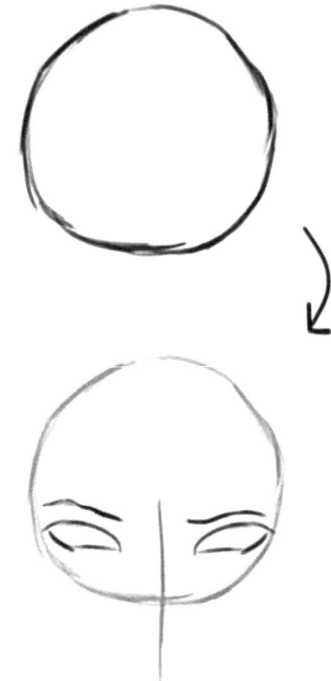

2. DRAW UP THE CHIN. IT SHOULD BE 1/3 OF THE WHOLE FACE. THE FIGURE SHOWS HOW TO MAKE A DETAILED DRAWING OF AN EYE WITH HIGHLIGHTS AND SHADING. DON'T FORGET ABOUT THE EYELASHES.

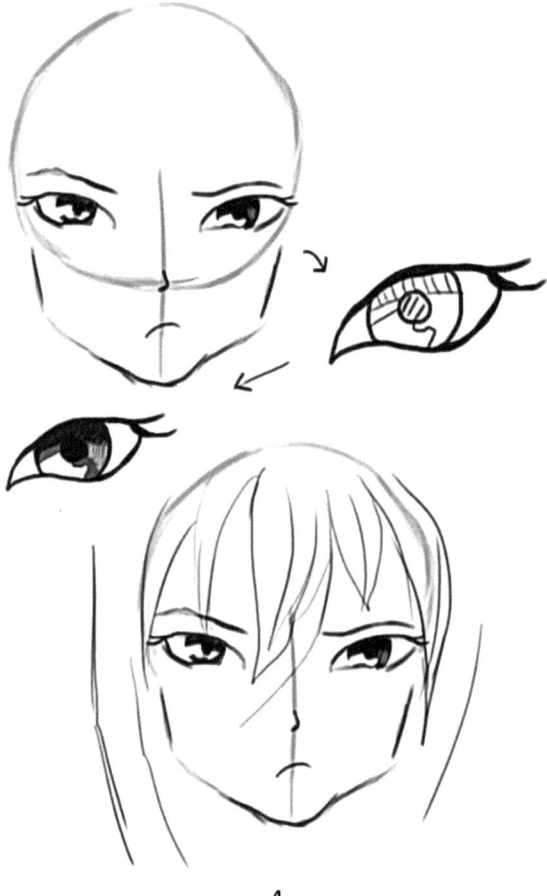

3. DRAW LOCKS OF HAIR. THEIR SHAPE AND DIRECTION SHOULD BE CHAOTIC, LIKE A REAL PERSON. YOU CAN ADD DEFINITION TO THE HAIR.

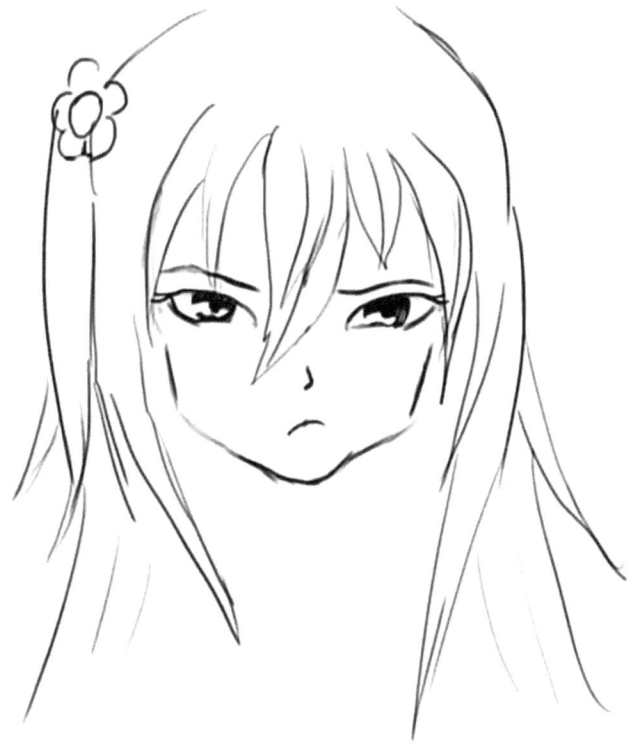

4. DRAW THE NECK AND SHOULDERS, AND THE DRAWING IS READY.

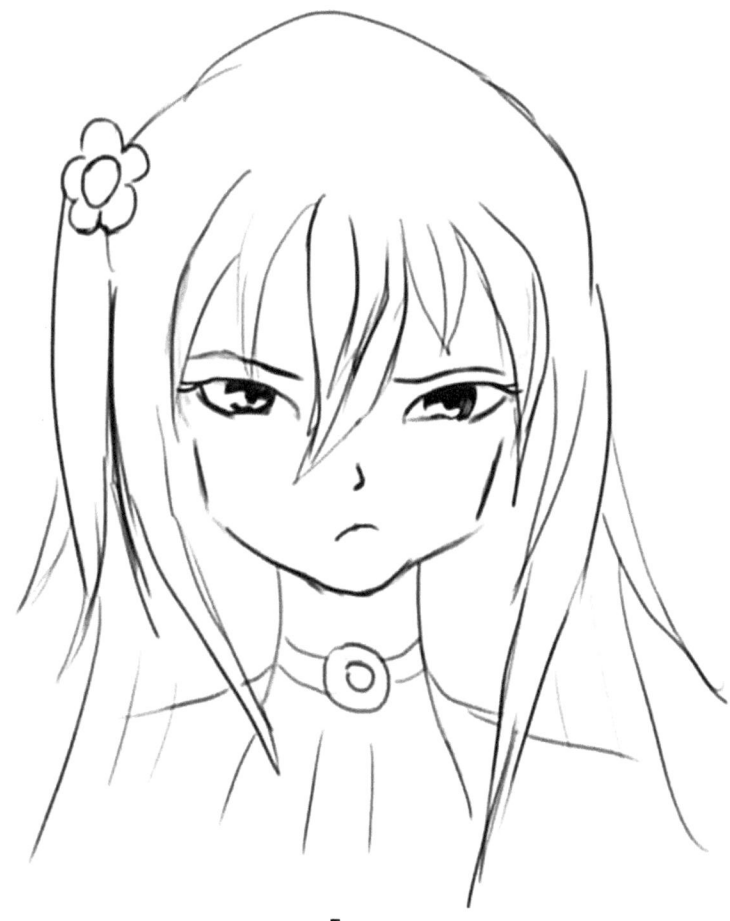

1. DRAW AN OVAL OF THE FACE WITH A CROSS. MARK THE MIDDLE OF THE FACE.

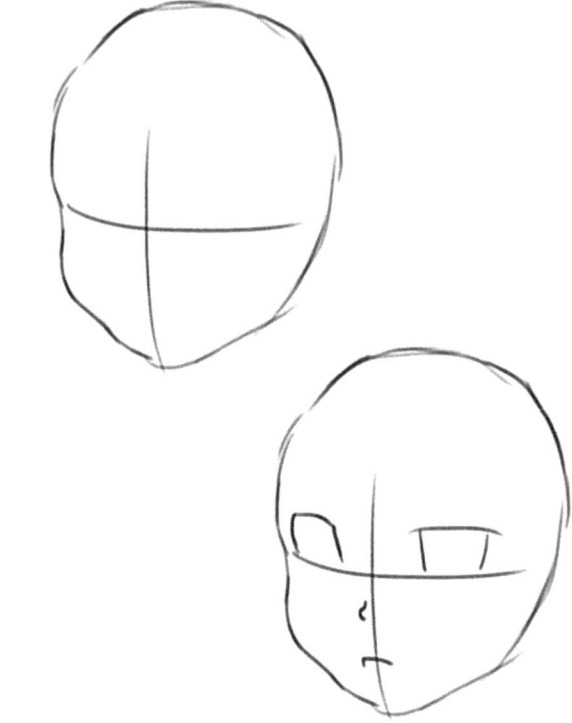

2. DRAW THE SHAPE OF THE EYE, NOSE, AND MOUTH.

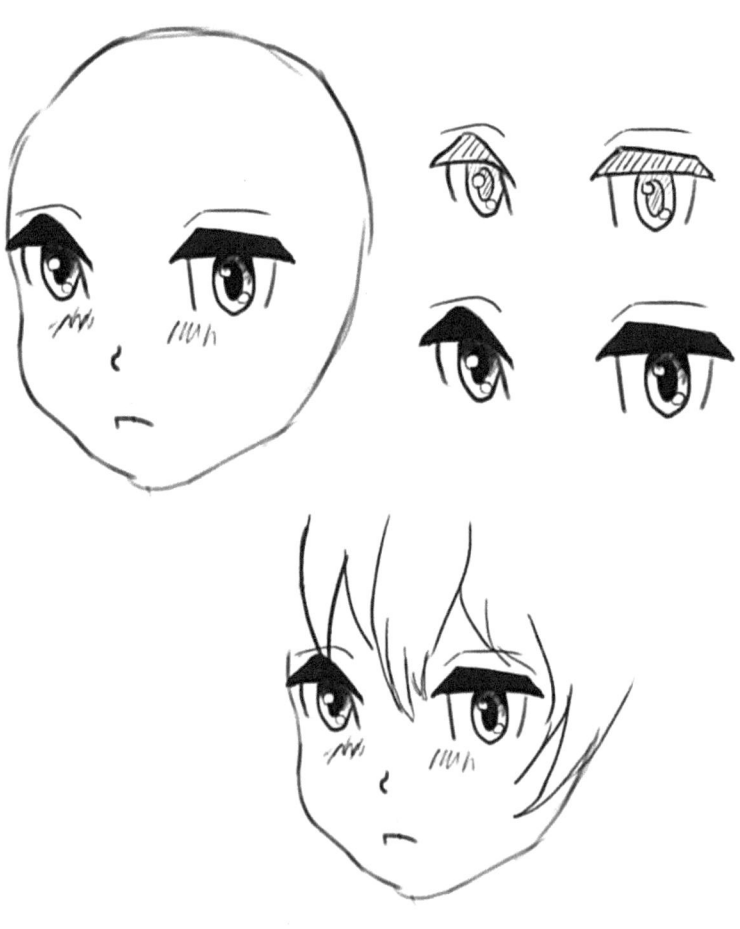

3. DRAW EYES IN DETAIL. EYELASHES SHOULD LOOK THINK AND HEAVY.
4. START TO DRAW HAIR.
5. DRAW THE STRANDS, THE EDGES, AND BLUSHING CHEEKS.

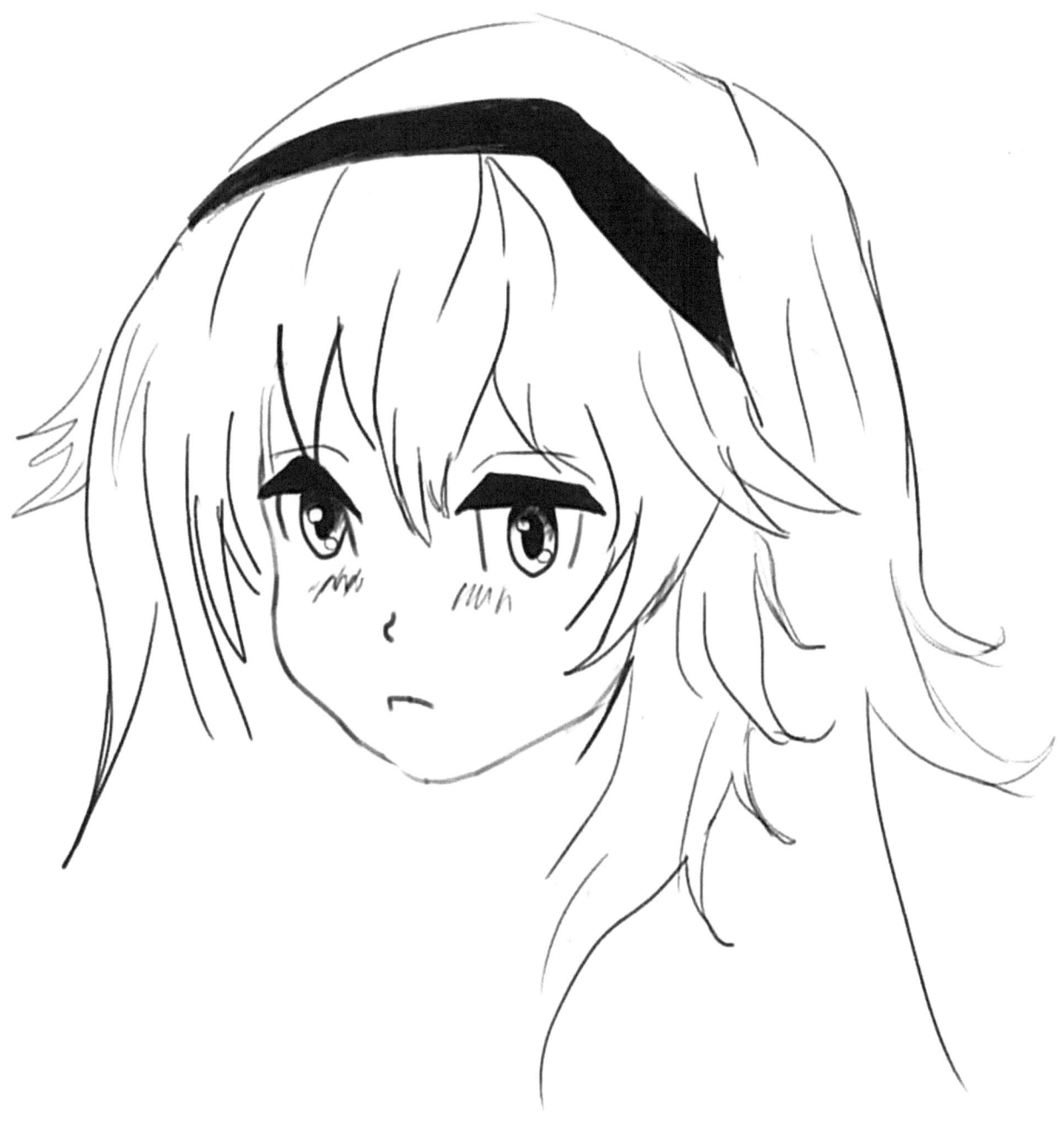

1. DRAW THE CONTOUR OF THE FACE.
2. MARK THE ESTIMATED MIDDLE OF THE FACE.

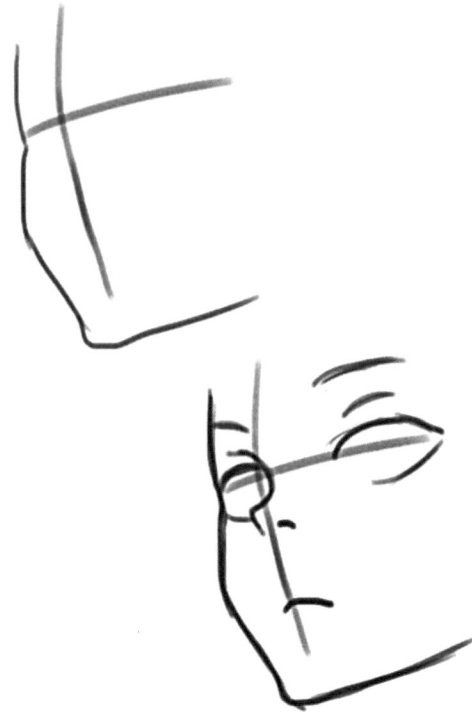

3. DRAW FACIAL FEATURES AND OUTLINE THE EYES IN DETAIL.

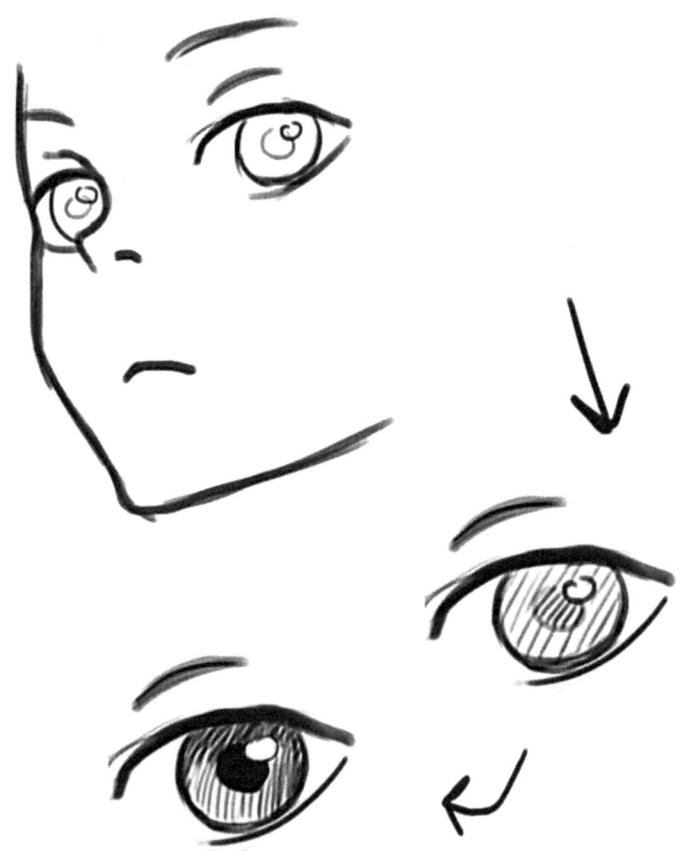

4. ADD HAIR.

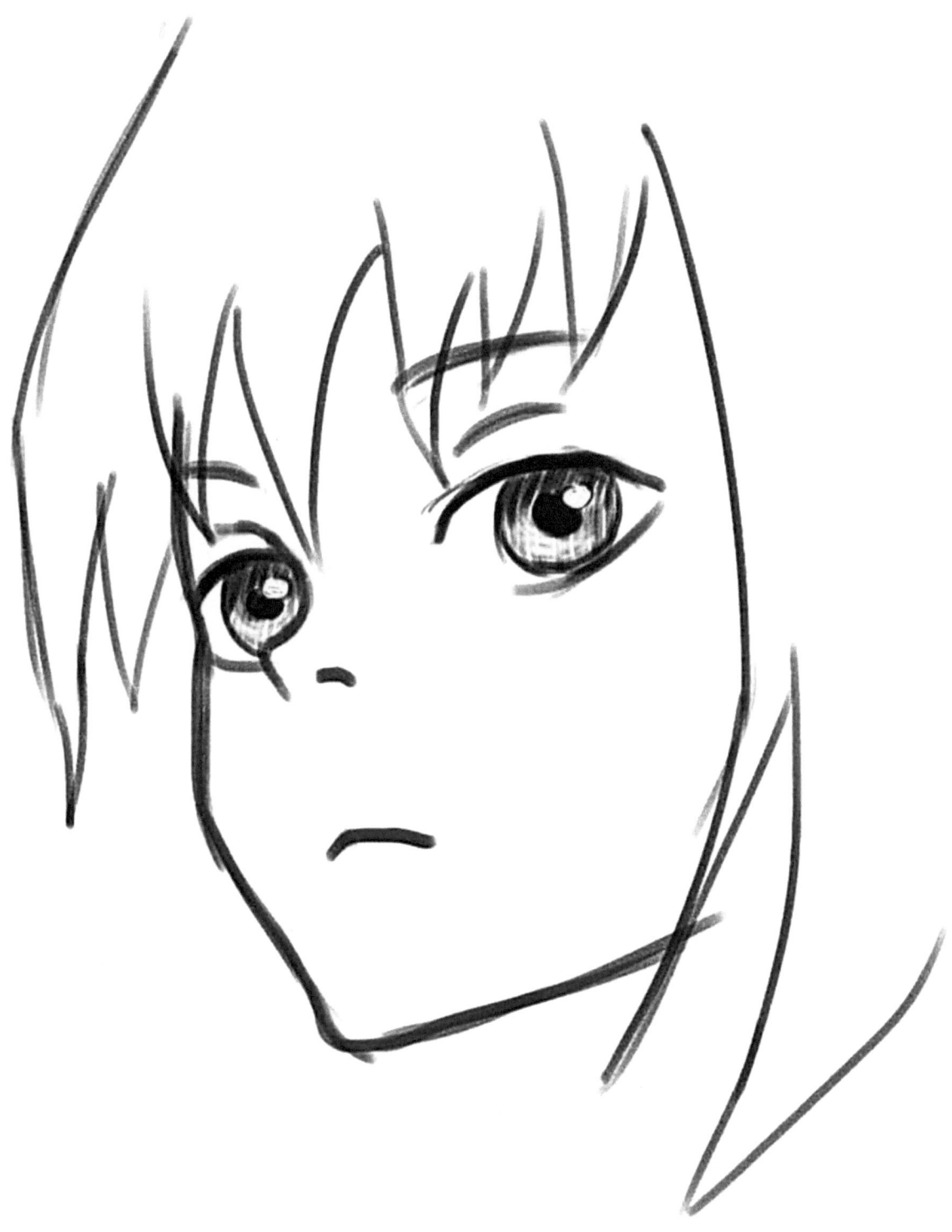

5. DRAW BANGS AND LOCKS OF HAIR. DON'T FORGET ABOUT THE RANDOMNESS IN THE DIRECTION OF THE STRANDS.

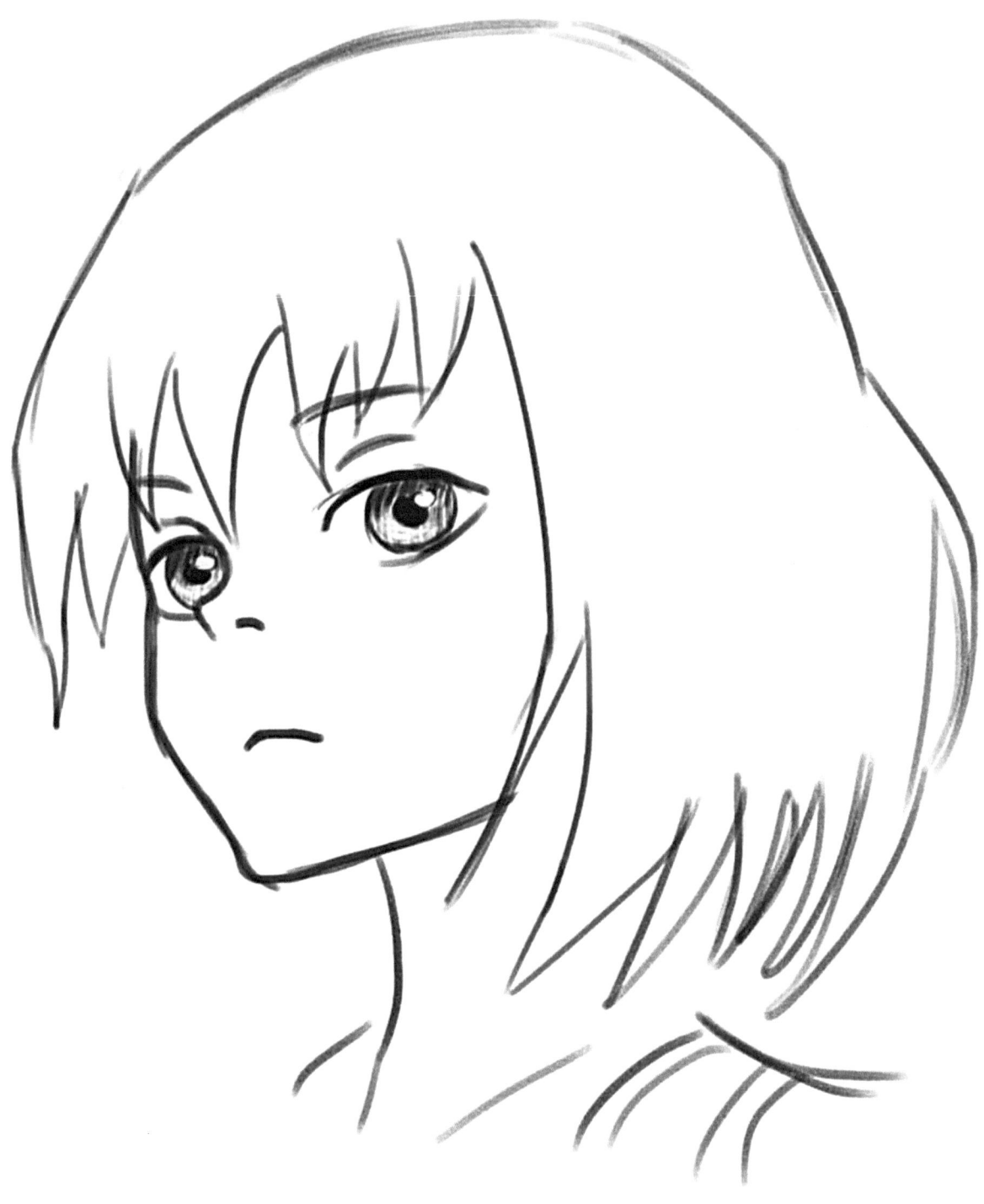

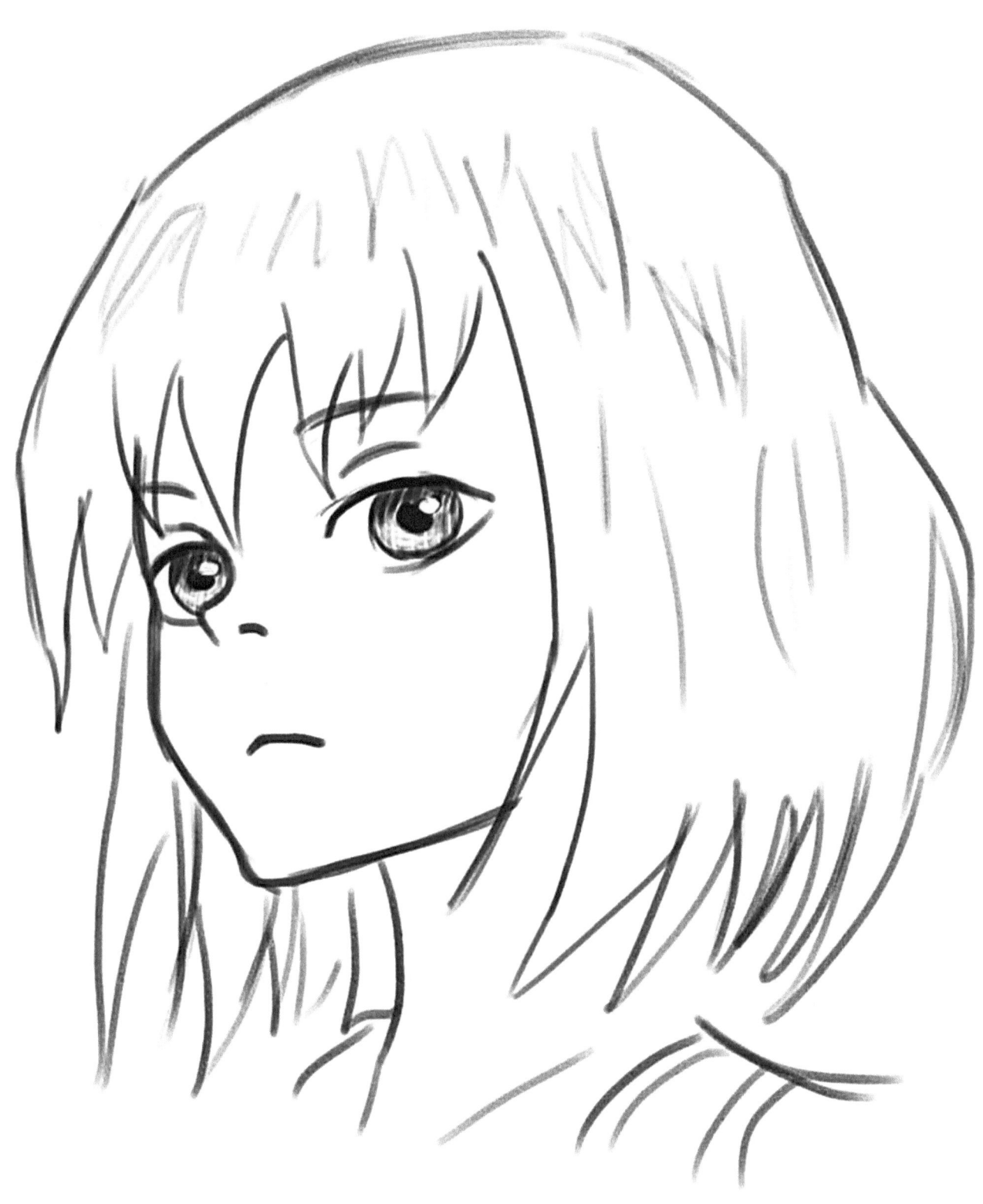

1. DRAW THE SHAPE OF THE FACE AND OUTLINE THE EYES, NOSE, AND MOUTH.

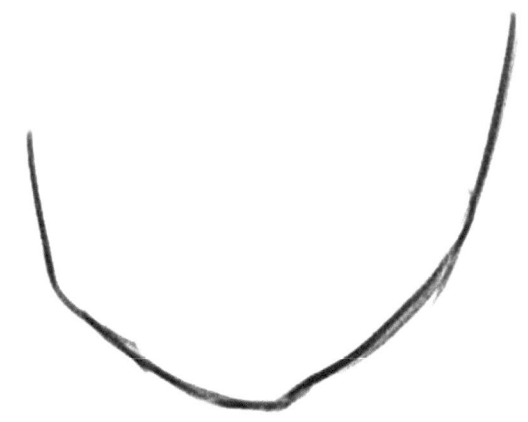

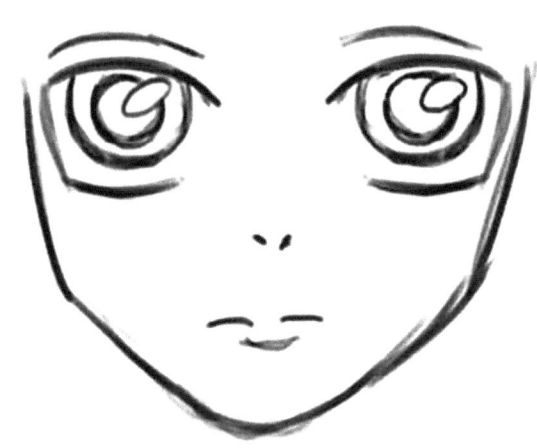

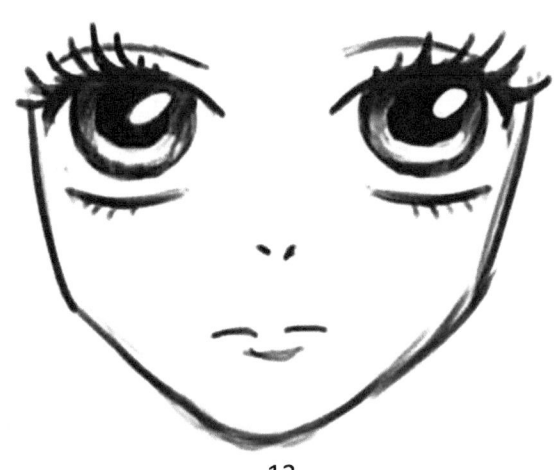

2. ELABORATE THE CHARACTER'S EYES.
3. DRAW HAIR, NECK, CLOTHES, AND COLLARBONES. ADD SHADING.

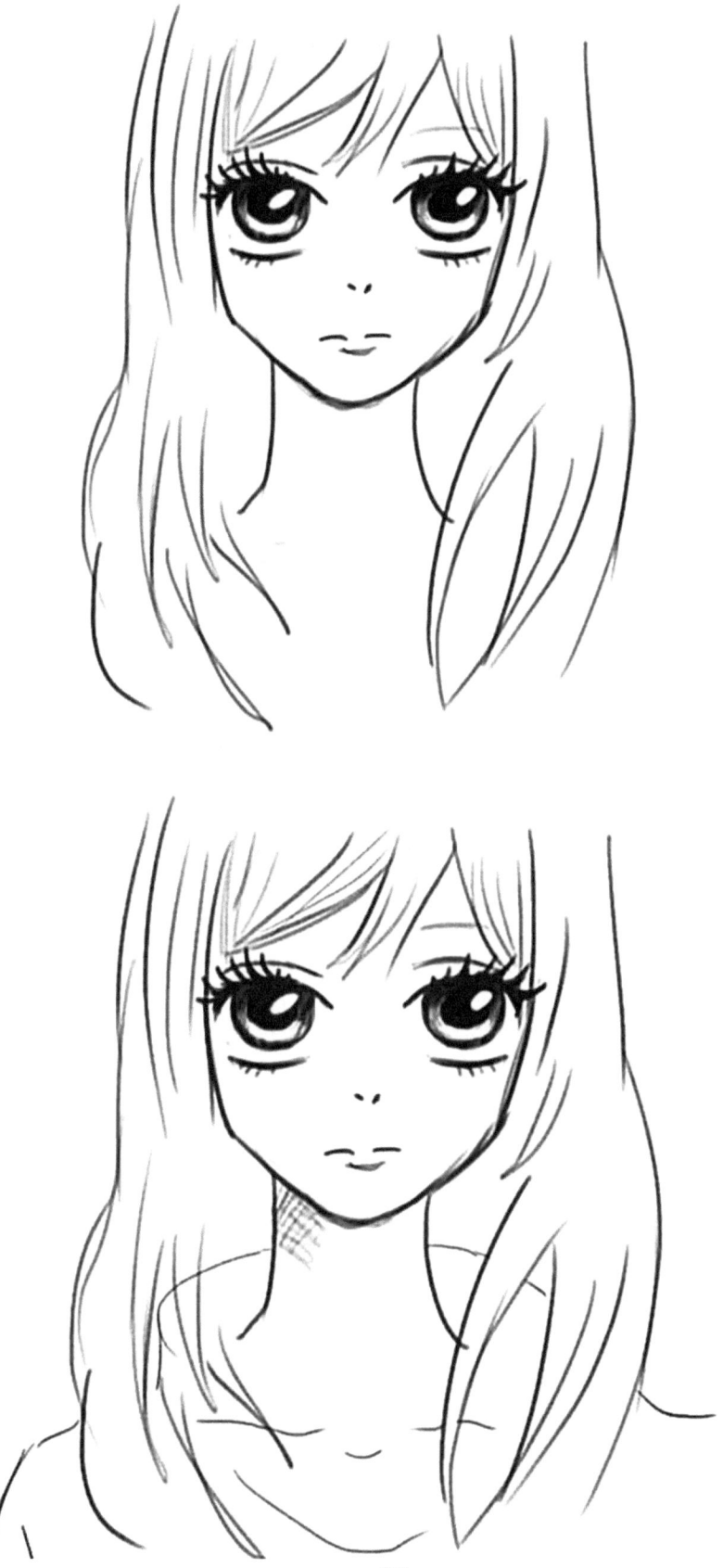

1. DRAW A CIRCLE AND DRAW A "SPINE" COMING DOWN FROM IT. ATTACH TO THE SPINE TO THE LIMBS.

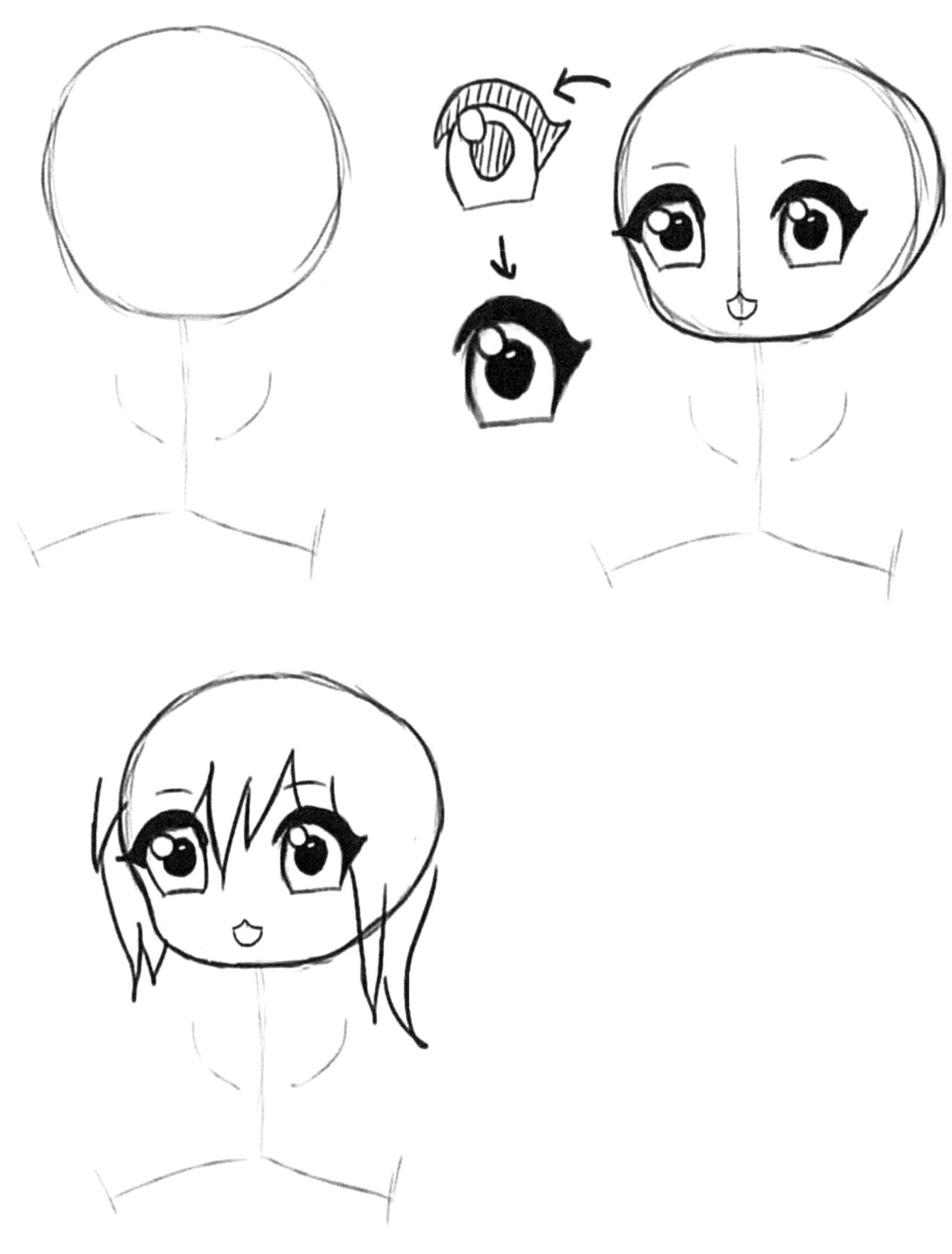

2. DRAW FACIAL FEATURES AND BEGIN TO DRAW HAIR.
3. ON THE HEAD, DRAW A HOOD WITH EARS. COMPLETE THE TORSO. PUT THE PACKAGE IN THE CHARACTER'S HANDS. DON'T FORGET ABOUT THE TAIL.

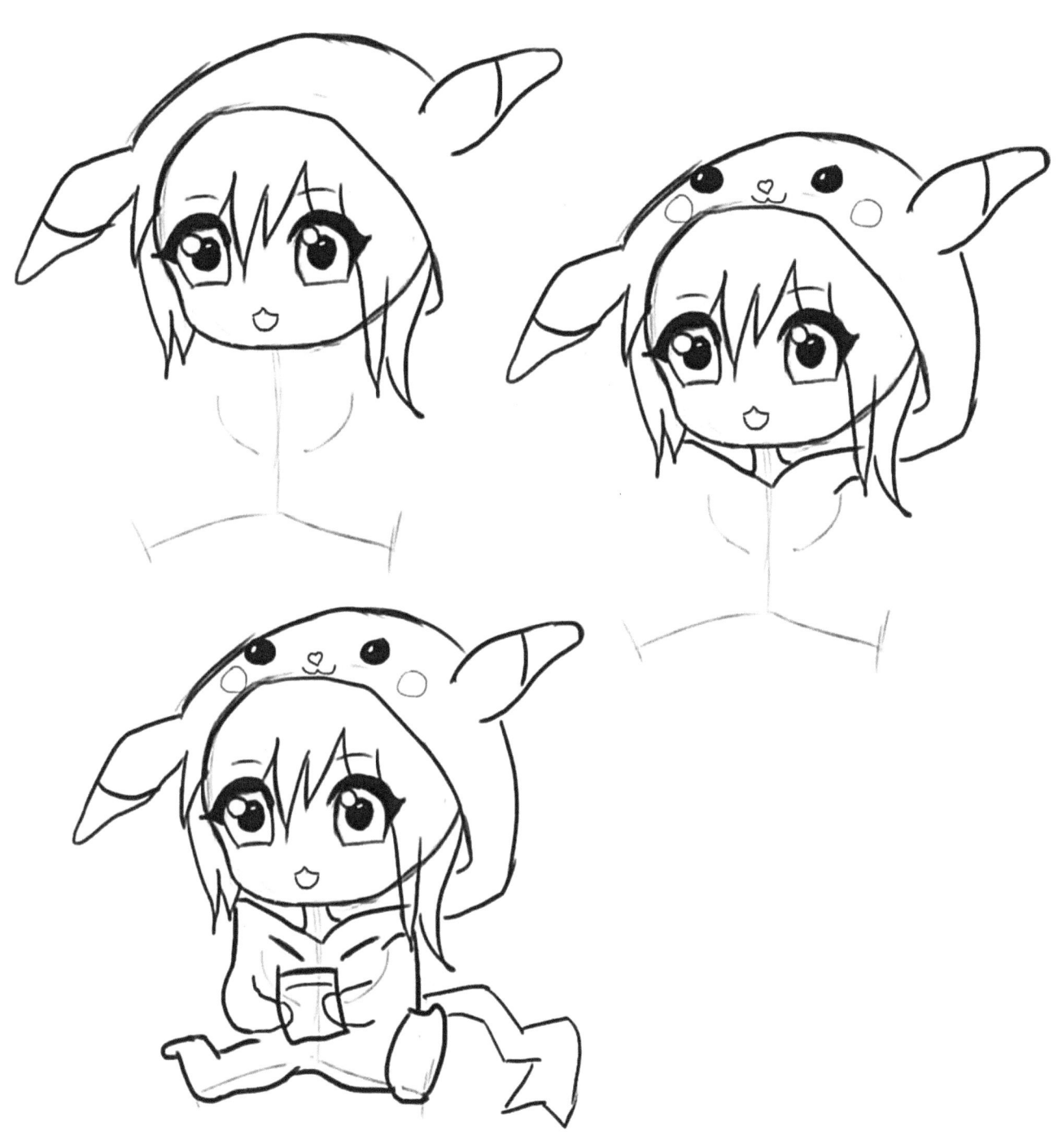

1. DRAW A HEAD, TRUNK, AND EXTREMITIES.

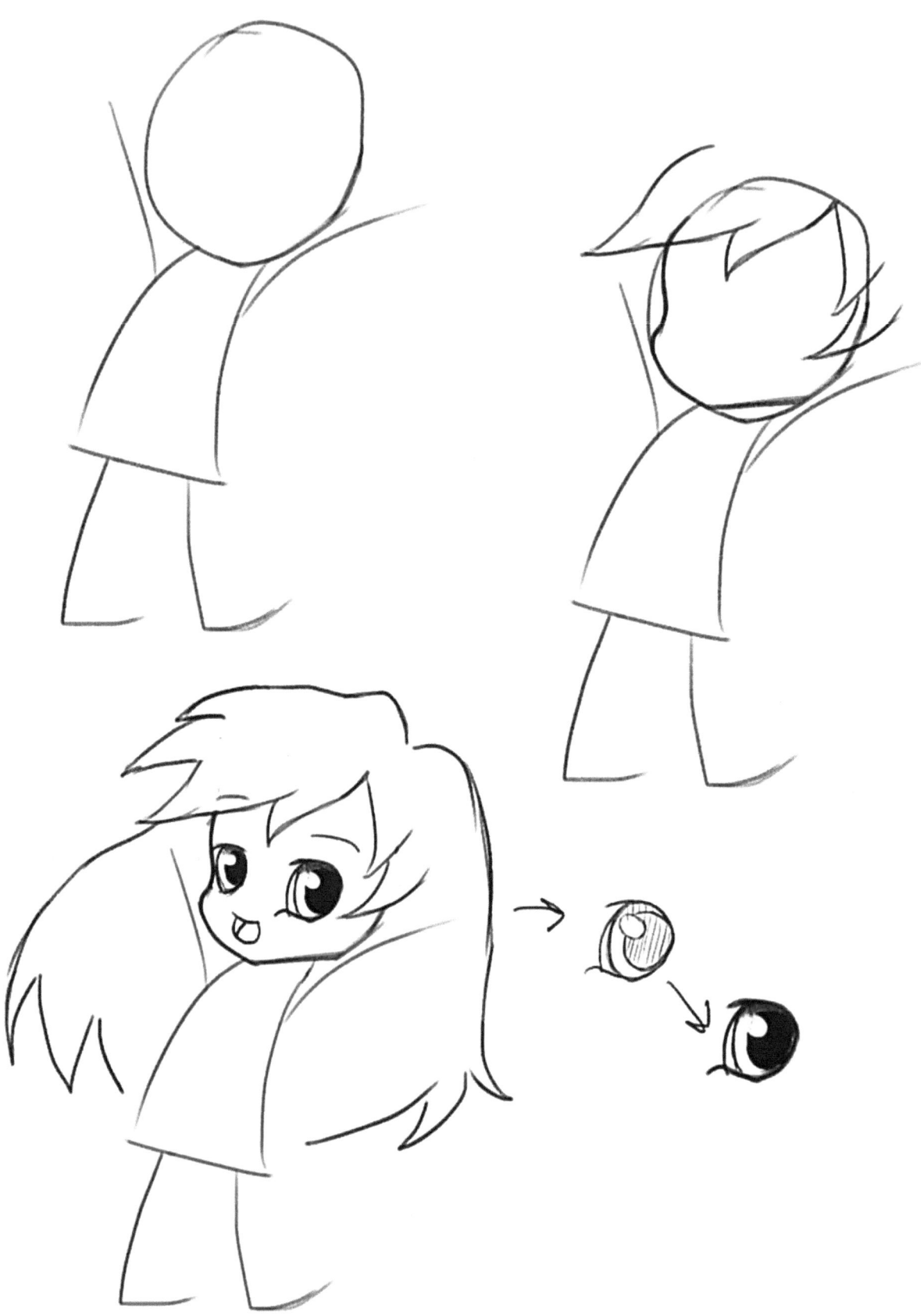

2. DRAW A MORE ACCURATE FACIAL SHAPE. EYES CAN BE DRAWN IN MORE DETAIL.
3. MOVE ON TO THE HAIR AND FACIAL FEATURES.
4. DRAW CLOTHES IN DETAIL, DRAWING ON OUR PREVIOUS WORKPIECES. DON'T FORGET ABOUT POCKETS, HAIR ACCESSORIES, AND SHOES. THE LITTLE DETAILS ARE IMPORTANT.

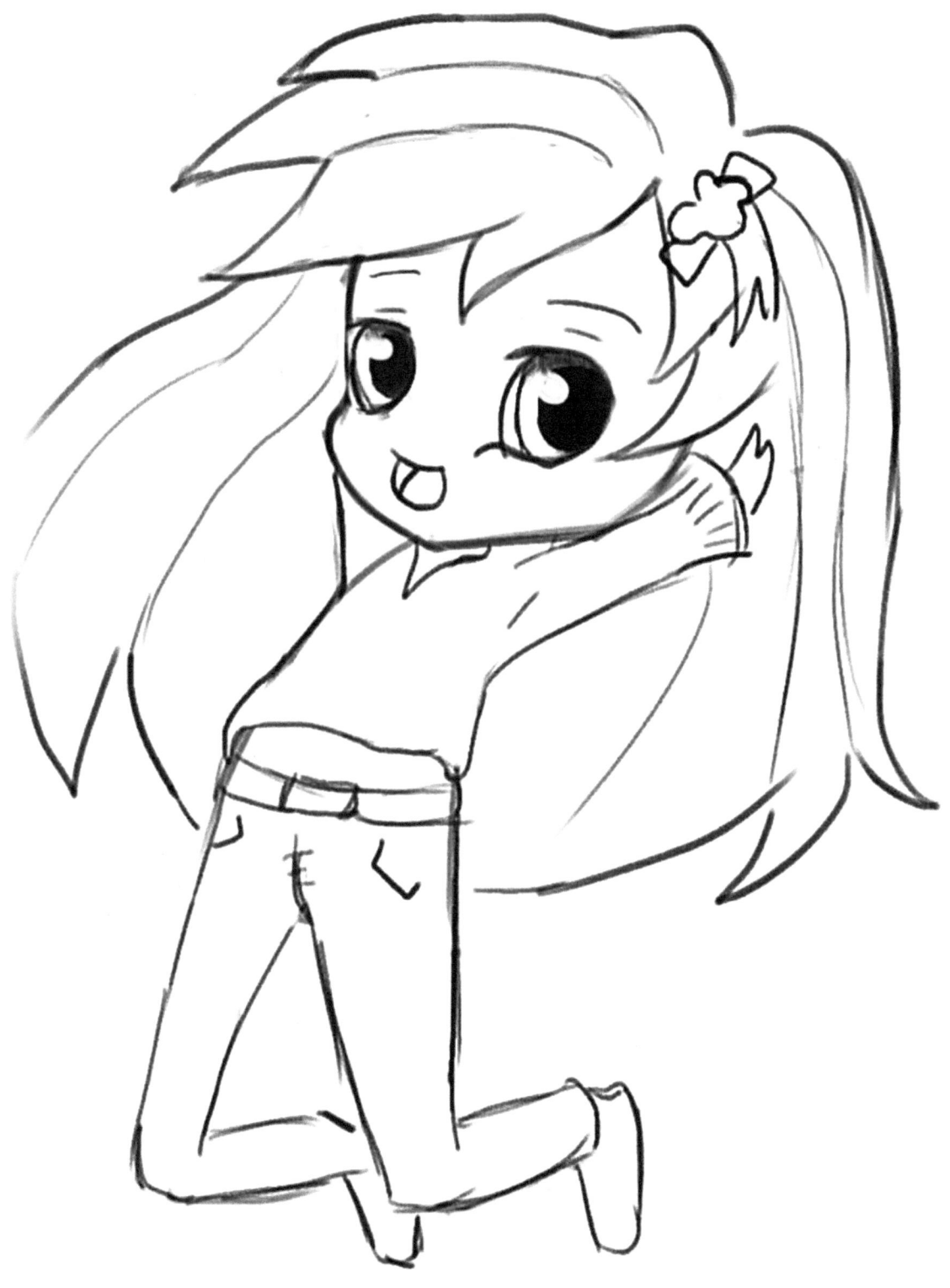

1. DRAW A BALL. WITH A CROSS-SHAPED SEGMENT, MARK THE MIDDLE OF THE FACE. DRAW A CHIN AND HAIR. TRY TO MAKE THE TIPS OF THE STRANDS POINTED.

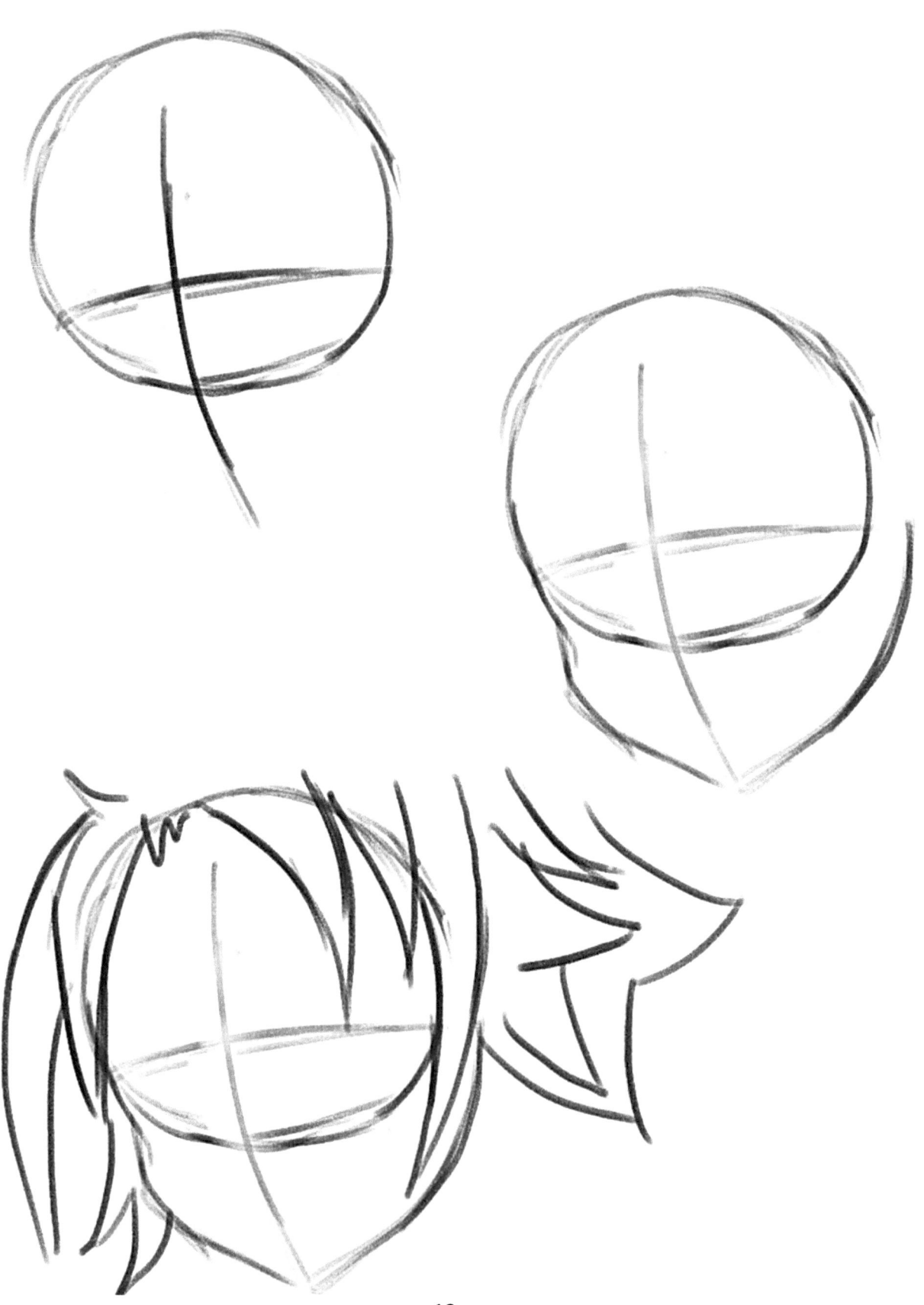

2. DRAW FACIAL FEATURES. ON EYES CLOSED WITH LAUGHTER, DON'T FORGET ABOUT THE EYELASHES. ADD HAIR AND AN EAR.
3. DRAW THE NECK. EVEN IF IT WON'T BE VISIBLE IN THE FINAL DRAWING, YOU NEED IT FOR DRAWING CLOTHES PROPERLY.

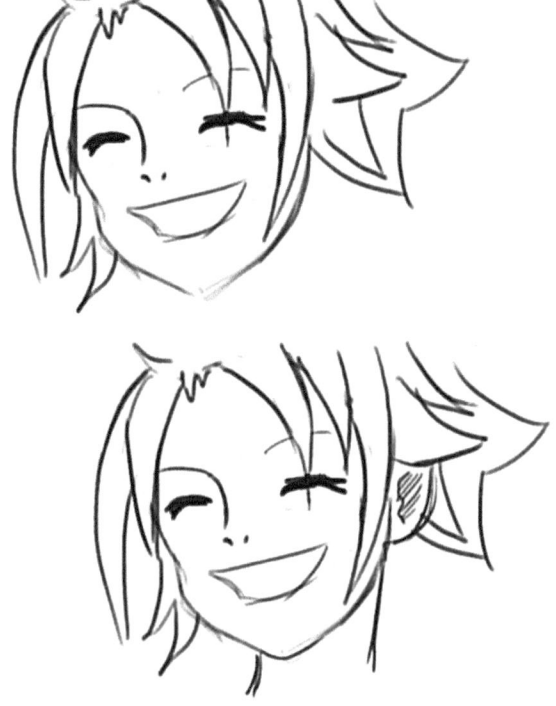

4. "DRESS UP" THE CHARACTER.
5. DRAW TEETH/SHADING ON CLOTHES, FACE.

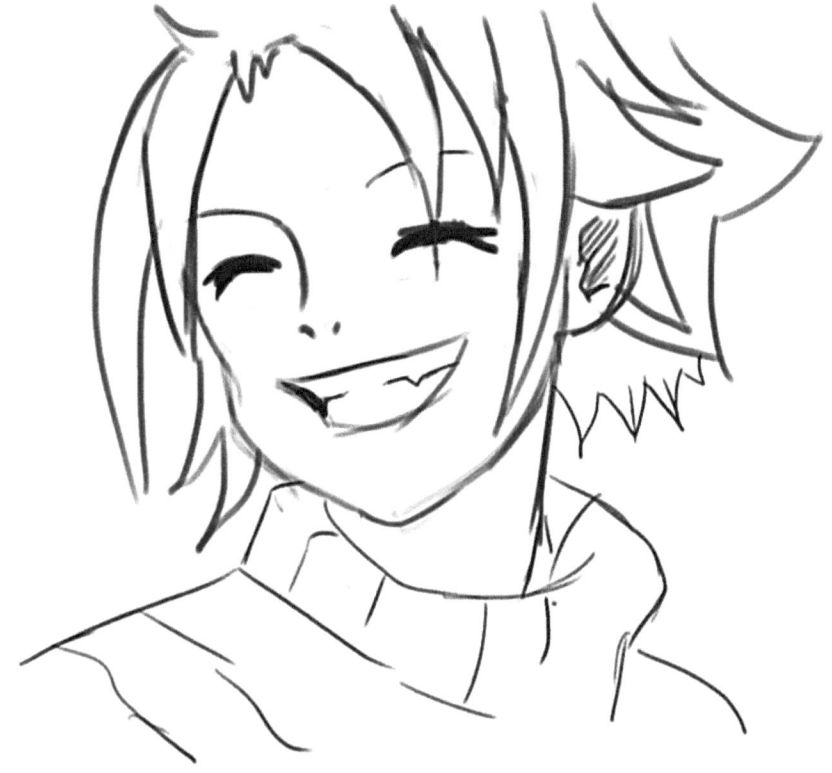

1. DRAW A HEAD. FROM THE HEAD WE DRAW A SMOOTH LINE OF THE "SPINE." MARK THE LINE OF THE SHOULDERS; FROM THE SHOULDERS, ATTACH ARMS THAT CROSS OVER ON THE CHEST. MARK SHOULDERS AND ELBOWS WITH CIRCLES.

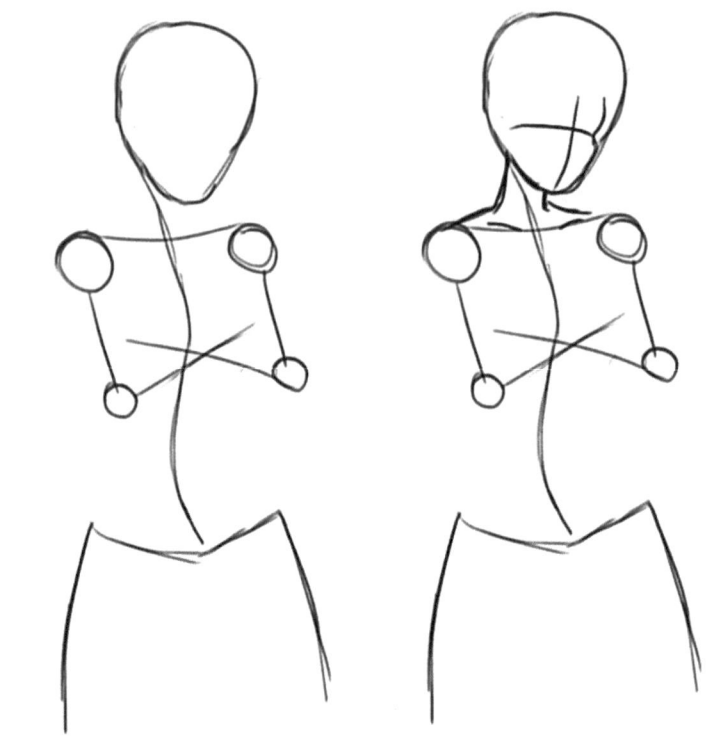

2. VERY CAREFULLY DRAW THE NECK, COLLARBONE, AND FACE SHAPE.

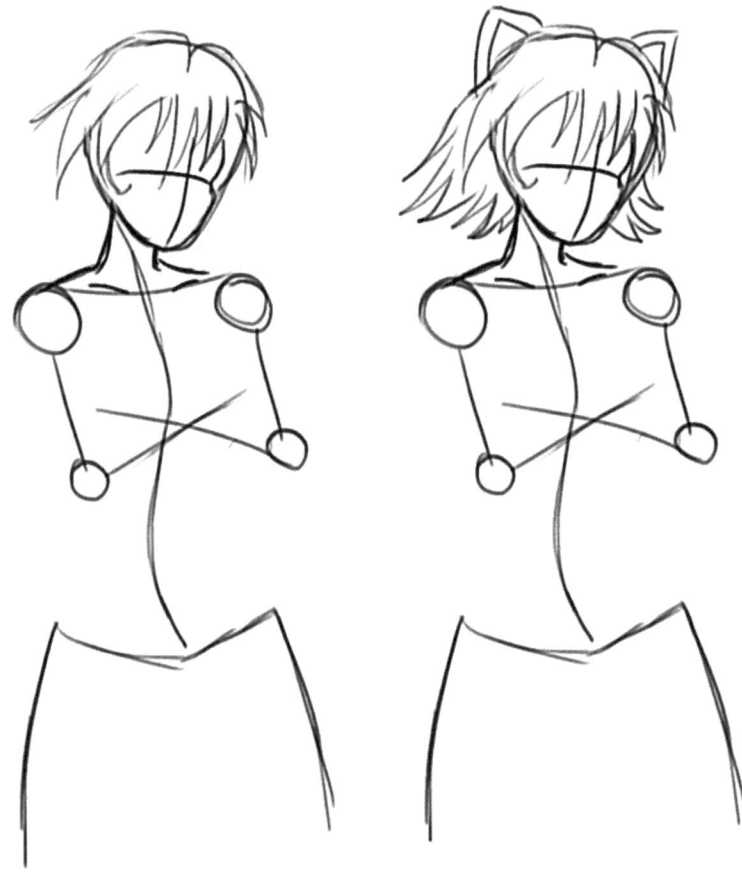

### 3. ADD DETAILS: HAIR AND ACCESSORIES.

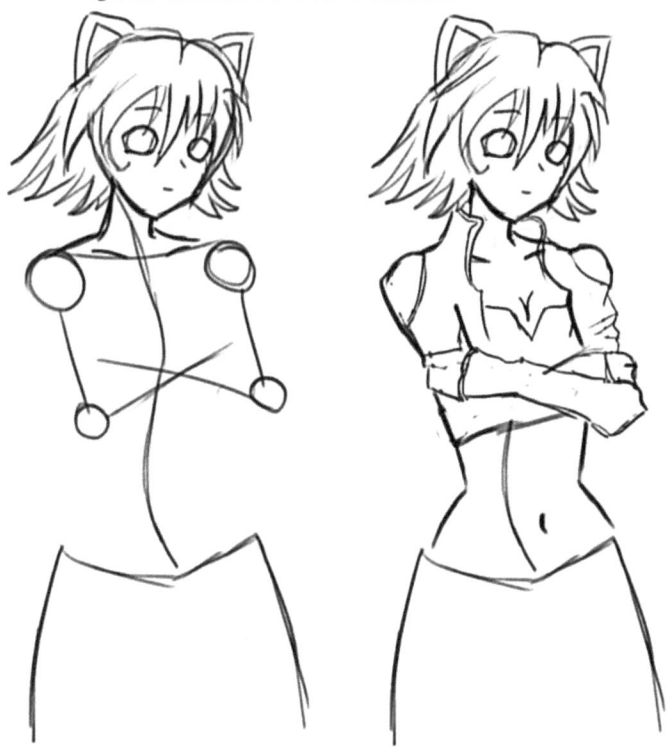

4. DRAW THE CHARACTER'S CLOTHES, HANDS, AND FACIAL FEATURES.
5. DRAW CLOTHES IN DETAIL. PAY SPECIAL ATTENTION TO THE EYES. DRAW A BUCKLE AND HOLES IN THE BELT.

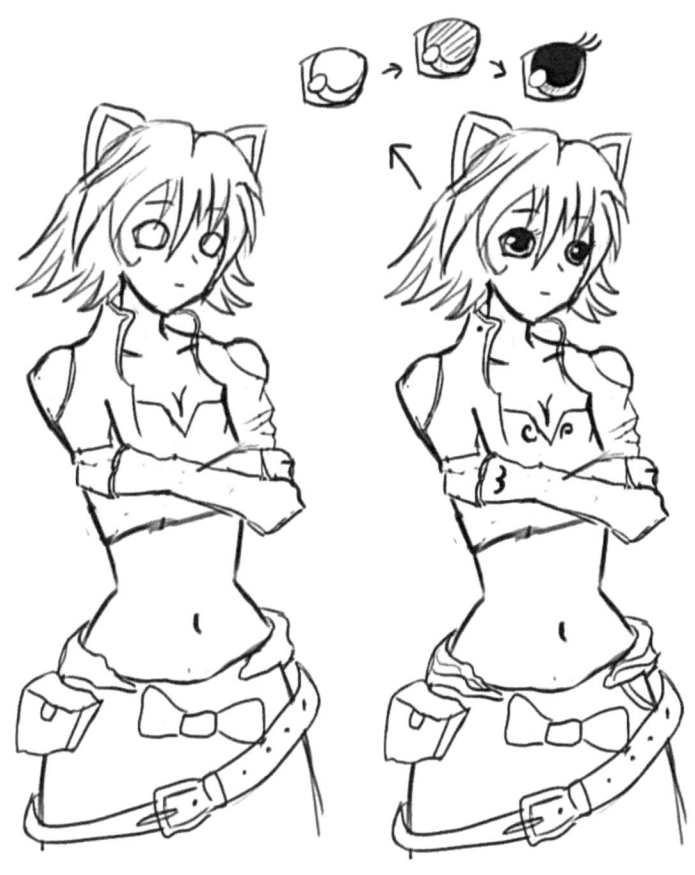

1. DRAW A FACE; FIND THE MIDDLE.
2. OUTLINE EYES AND EYEBROWS.
3. FINISH THE HAIR AND TORSO.

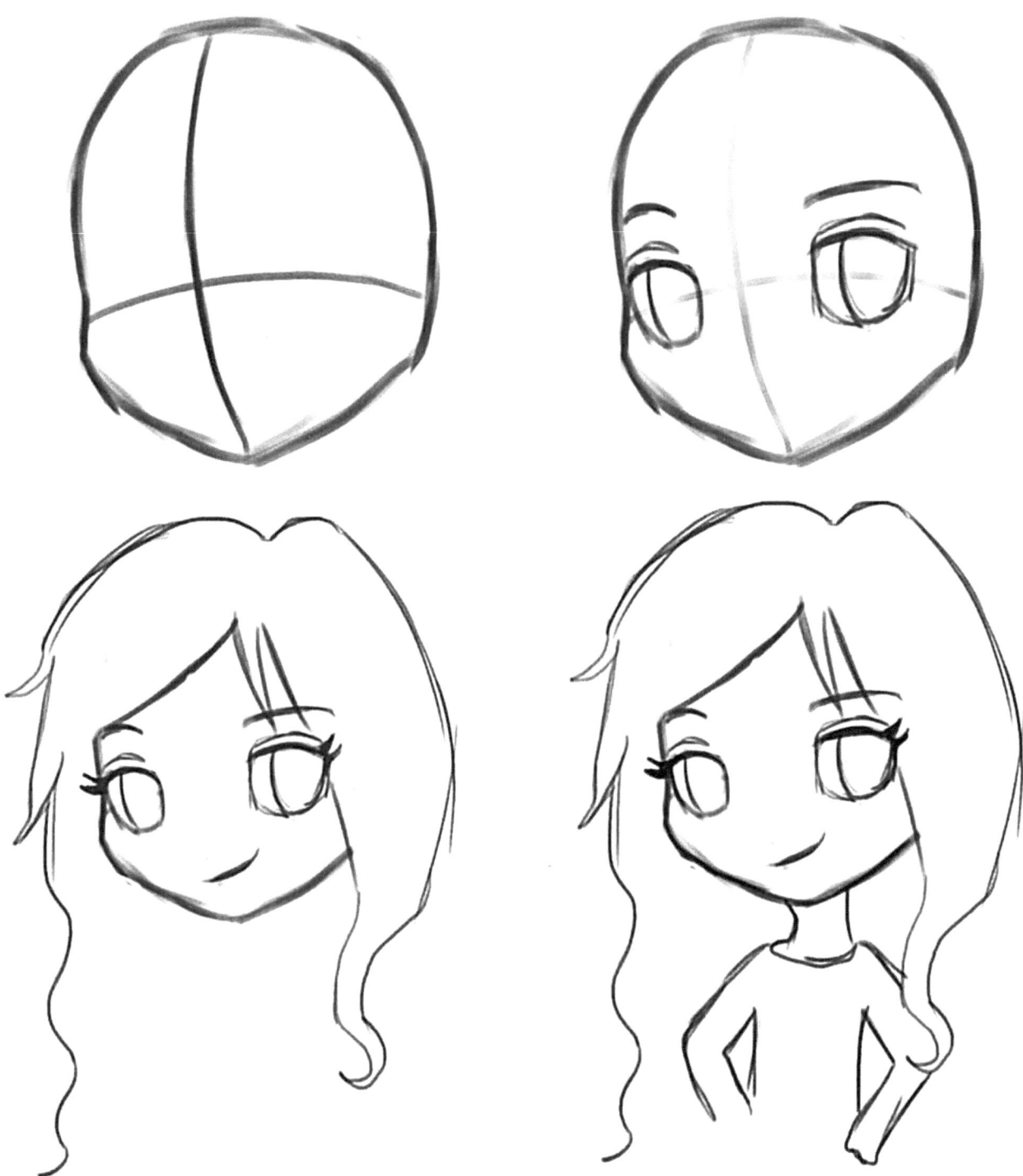

4. DRAW LEGS. THE TORSO AND LEGS ARE THE WORKPIECE.
5. NOW ON OUR BLANK, DRAW PARTS, CLOTHES, AND SHOES. GO FURTHER TO DRAW THE HAIR IN MORE DETAIL, AND ADD DEFINITION TO THE HAIR.

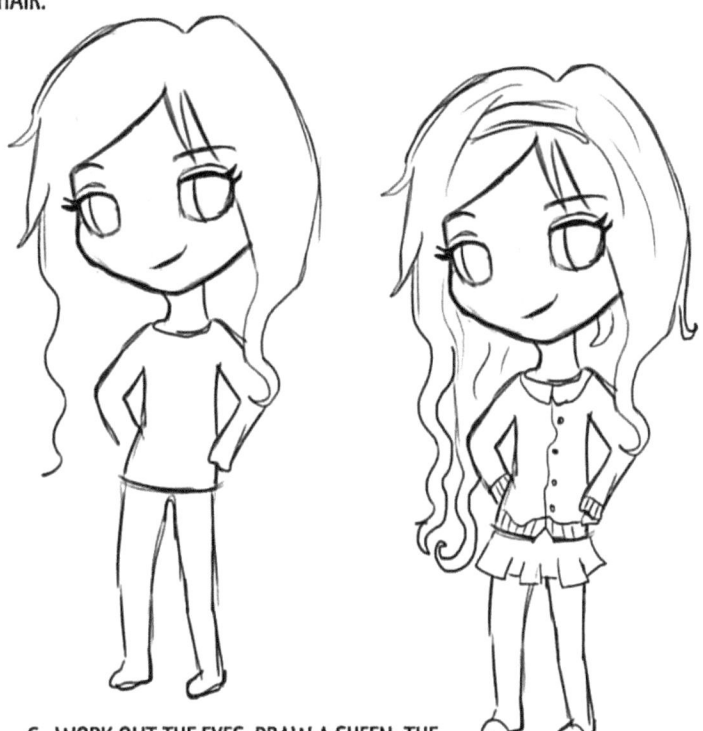

6. WORK OUT THE EYES: DRAW A SHEEN, THE PUPILS, AND DO NOT FORGET ABOUT THE EYELASHES.
7. ADD A CAT TO THE PICTURE.

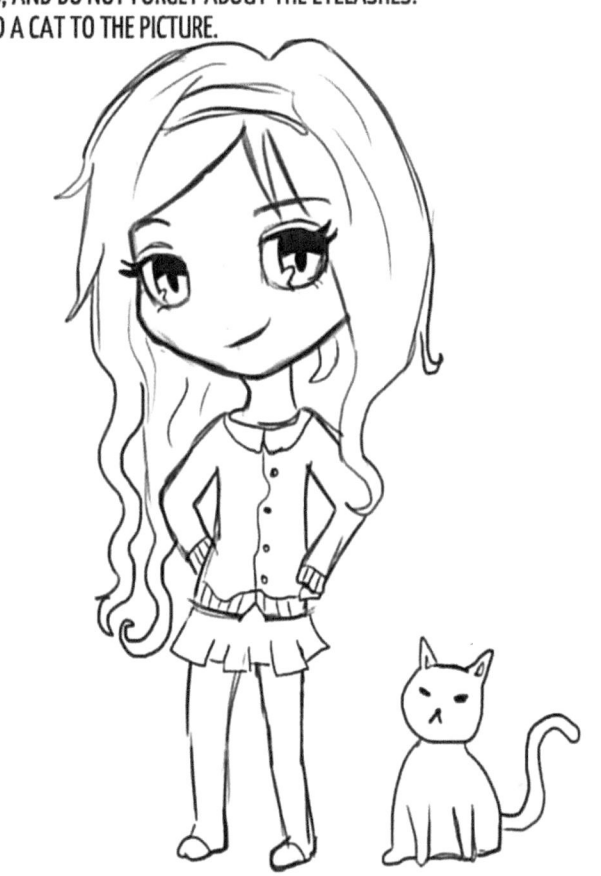

1. THIS PATTERN IS COMPLICATED; BE SURE TO COPY EACH LINE PRECISELY SO THAT THE FINAL PATTERN DOESN'T END UP CURVED.

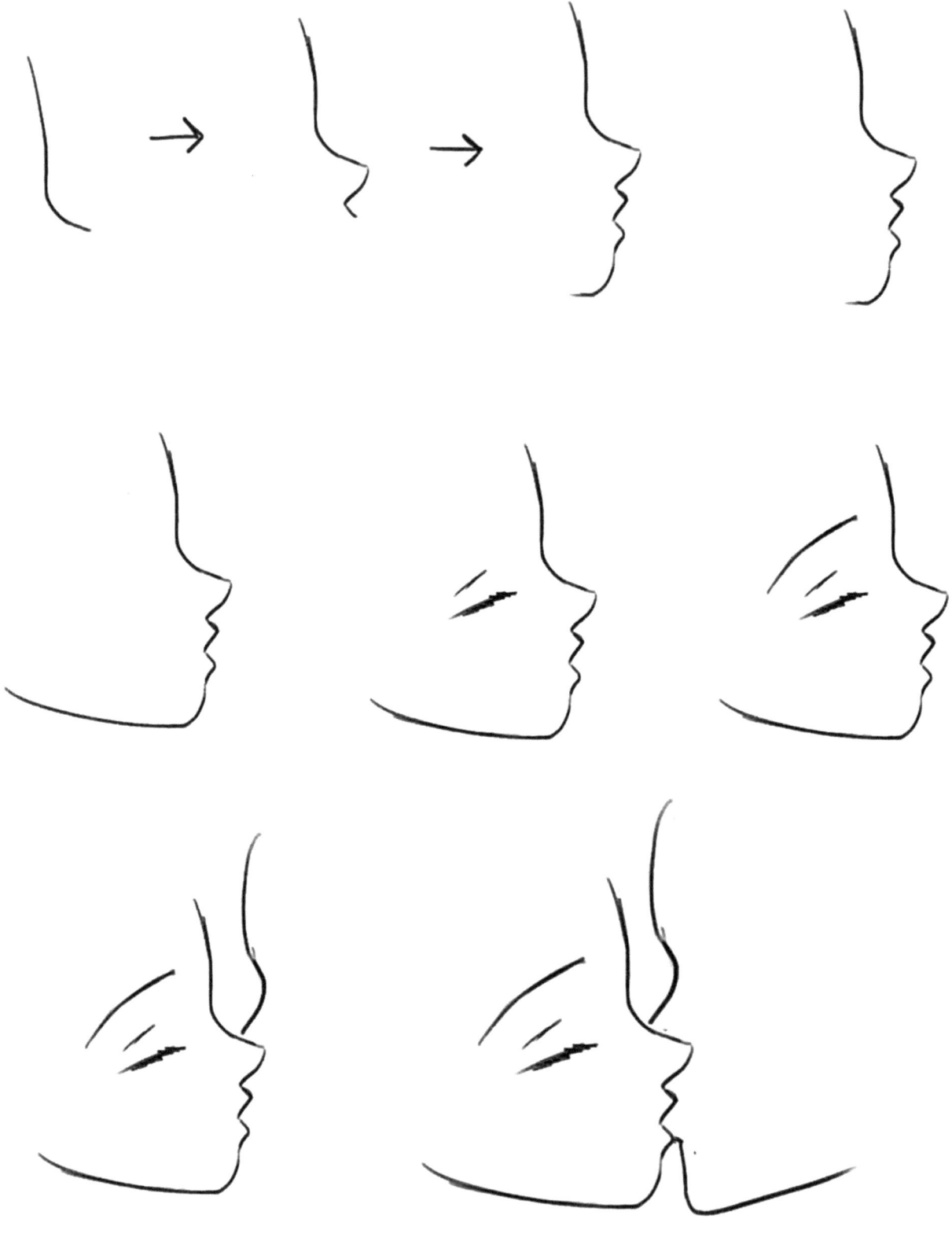

2. DRAW THE FACE SHAPE OF THE GIRL AS SHOWN IN THE FIGURE, AND PROCEED TO THE OUTLINES OF THE GUY.

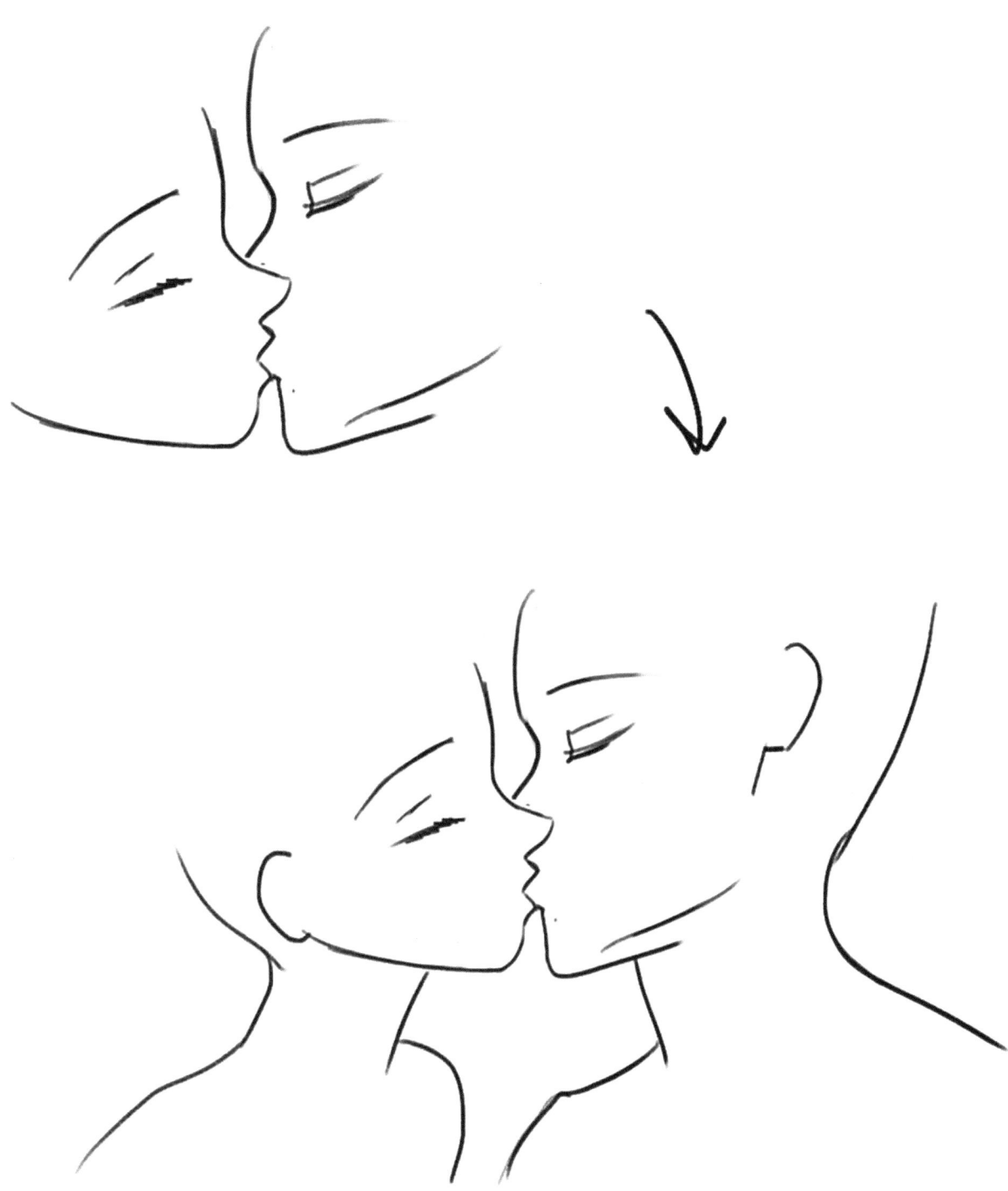

3. DRAW A LINE ON THE GUY'S CHIN TO INDICATE THE ANGLE.
4. DRAW NECKS, SHOULDERS, AND EARS.

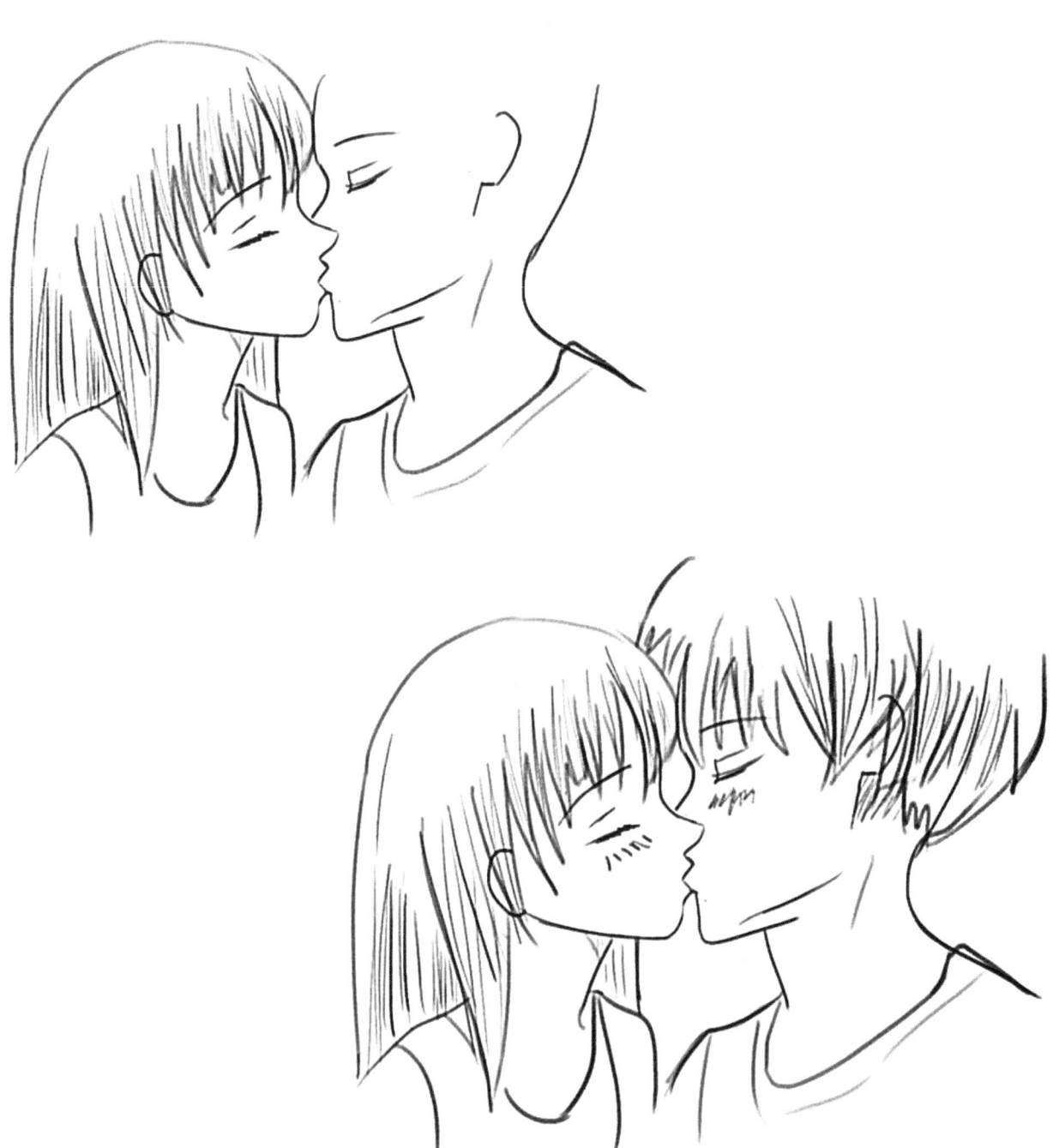

5. COMPLETE THE DRAWING WITH BOTH CHARACTERS' HAIR AND APPLY CHIAROSCURO.

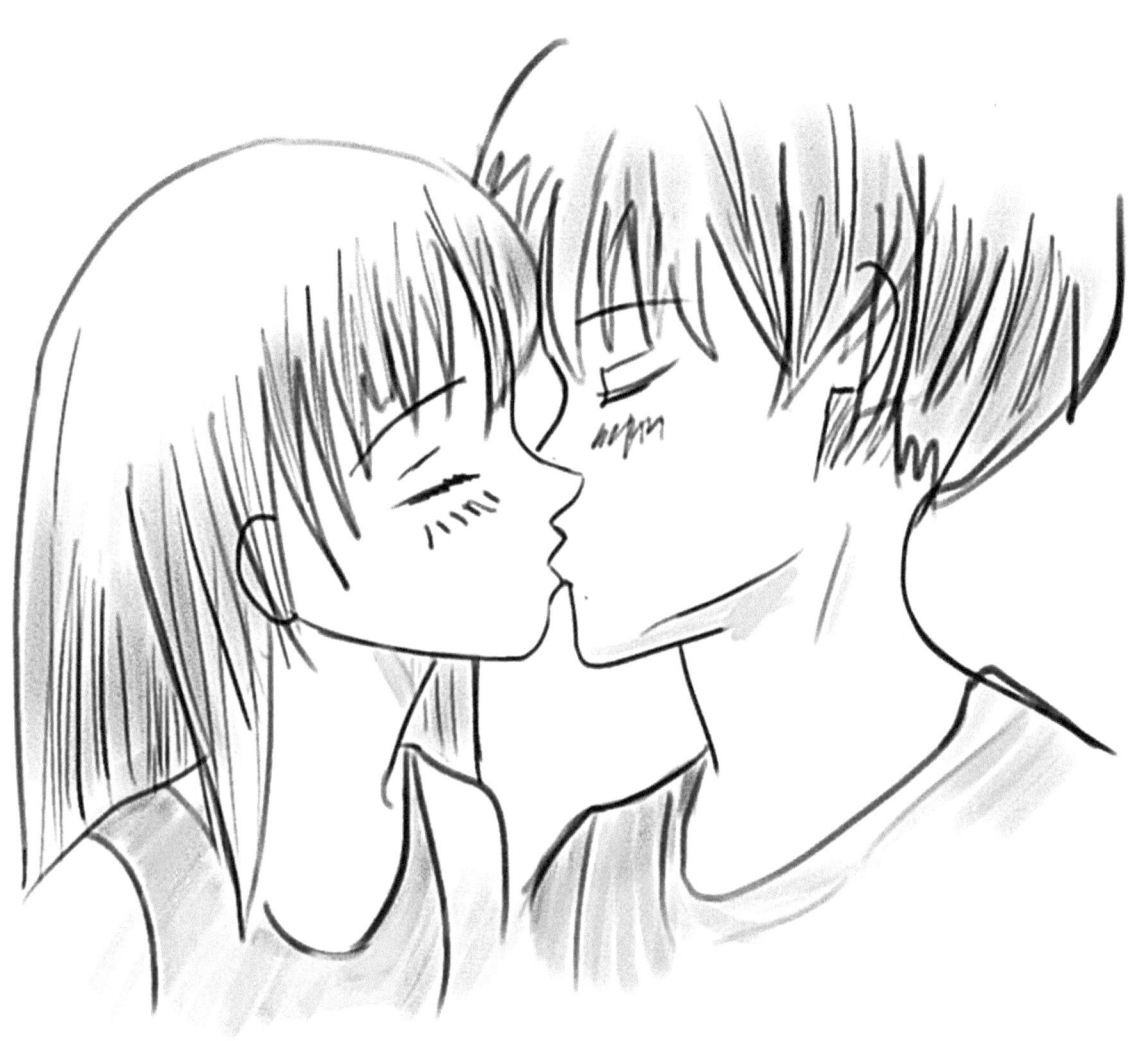

1. DRAW THE FACE; FIND THE MIDDLE.
2. ON THE TOP, DRAW BANGS AND LOCKS OF HAIR.
3. ERASE THE MARKUP AND DRAW FACIAL FEATURES: EYES, NOSE, AND MOUTH.

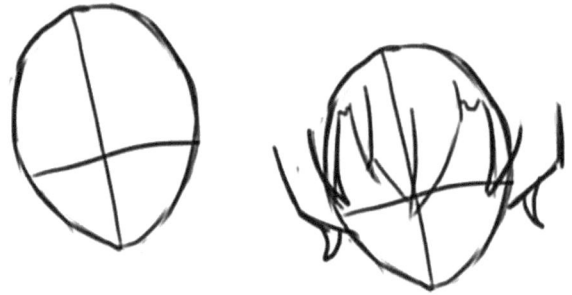

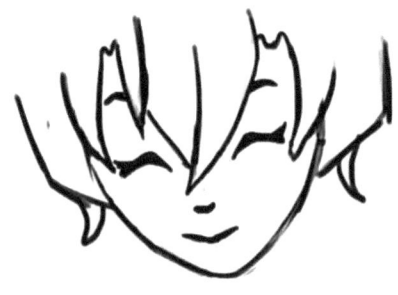

4. FINISH THE HEAD.

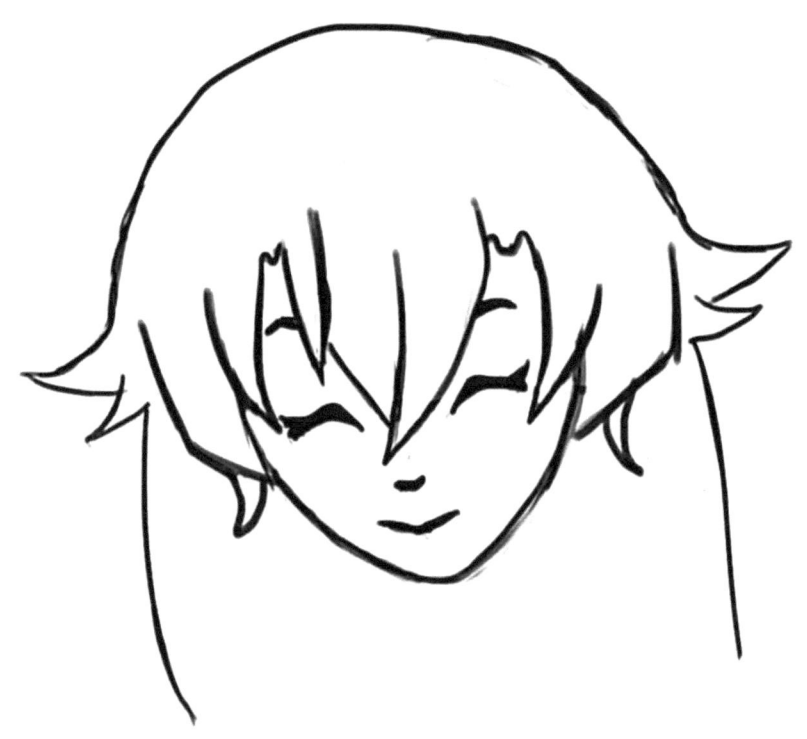

5. ADD ACCESSORIES TO THE HAIR. FINISH THE NECK, SHOULDERS, AND COLLARBONES.

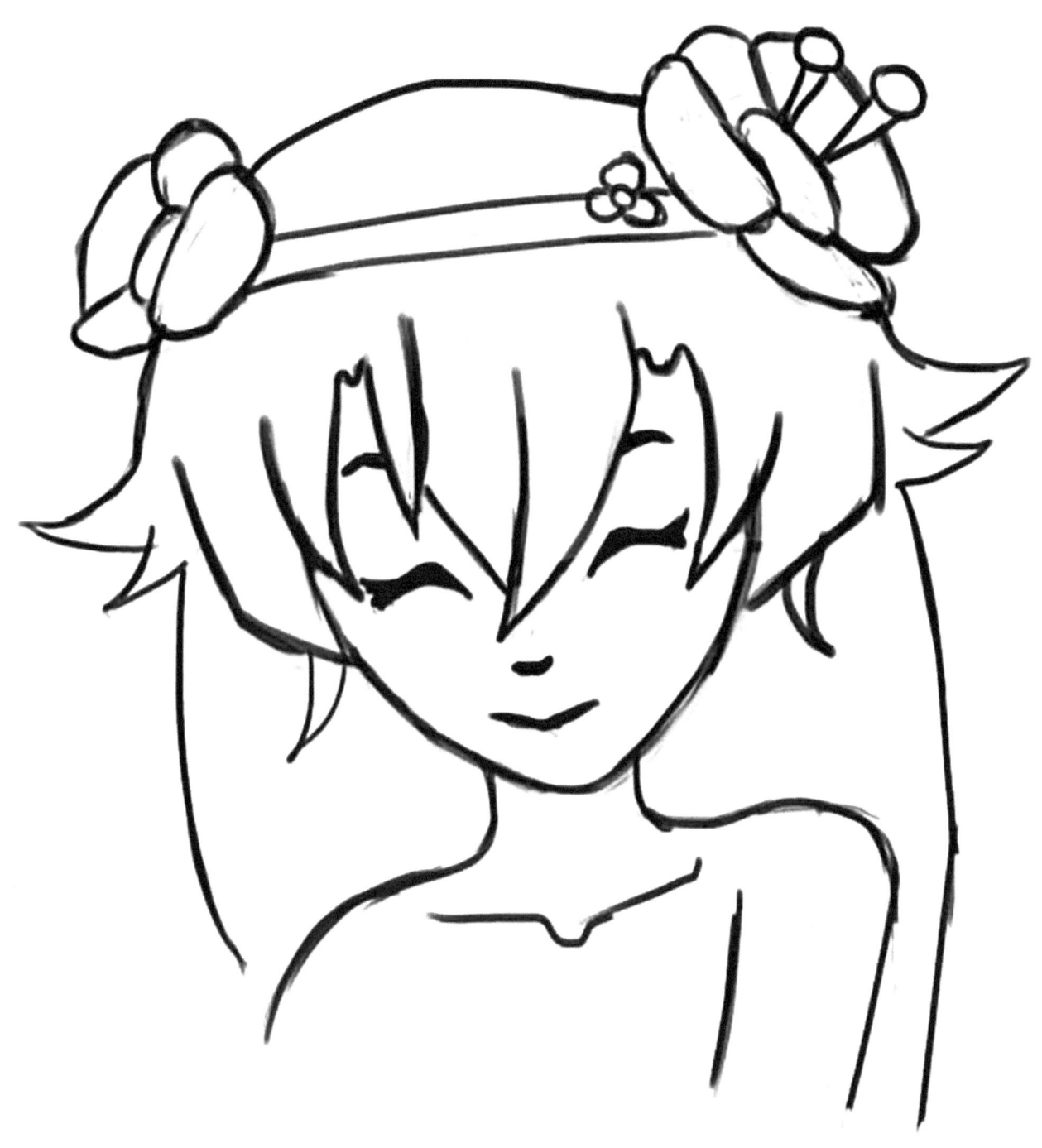

1. DRAW THREE SEGMENTS. THE DISTANCE BETWEEN WHICH SHOULD BE THE SAME.
2. INSIDE, DRAW TWO IDENTICAL BALLS.
3. OUTLINE THE CHEEK AND FOREHEAD. IN THE DIRECTION OF THE BALL, DRAW THE BODY AS SHOWN IN THE FIGURE.

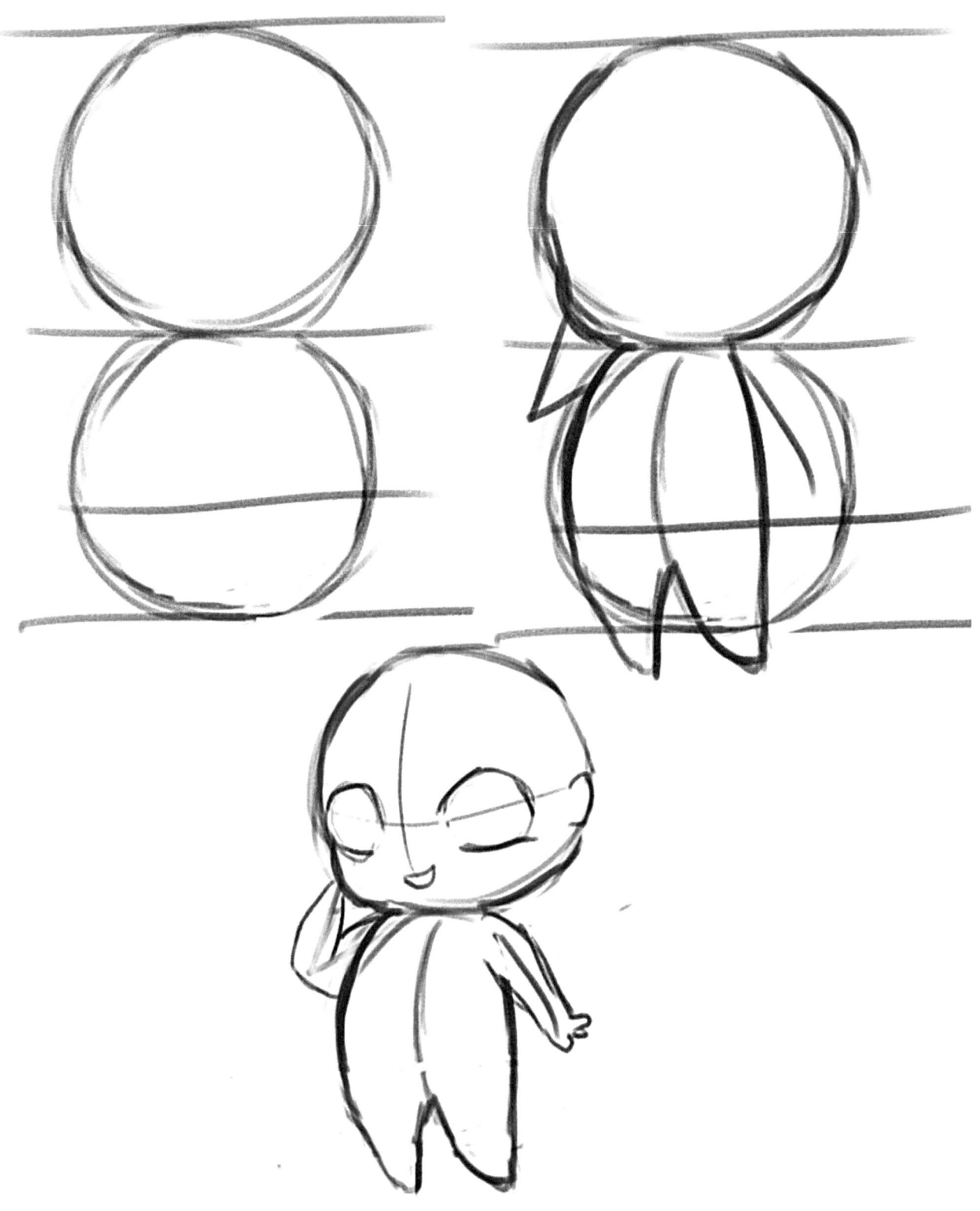

4. WIPE OFF EXCESS. ADD EYES AND DRAW HANDS AND FACIAL FEATURES.
5. "DRESS UP" THE CHARACTER. DRAW A HAIRSTYLE, PUPILS, AND EYE SHEEN.
6. ADD THE SHADING, AND THE PICTURE IS READY.

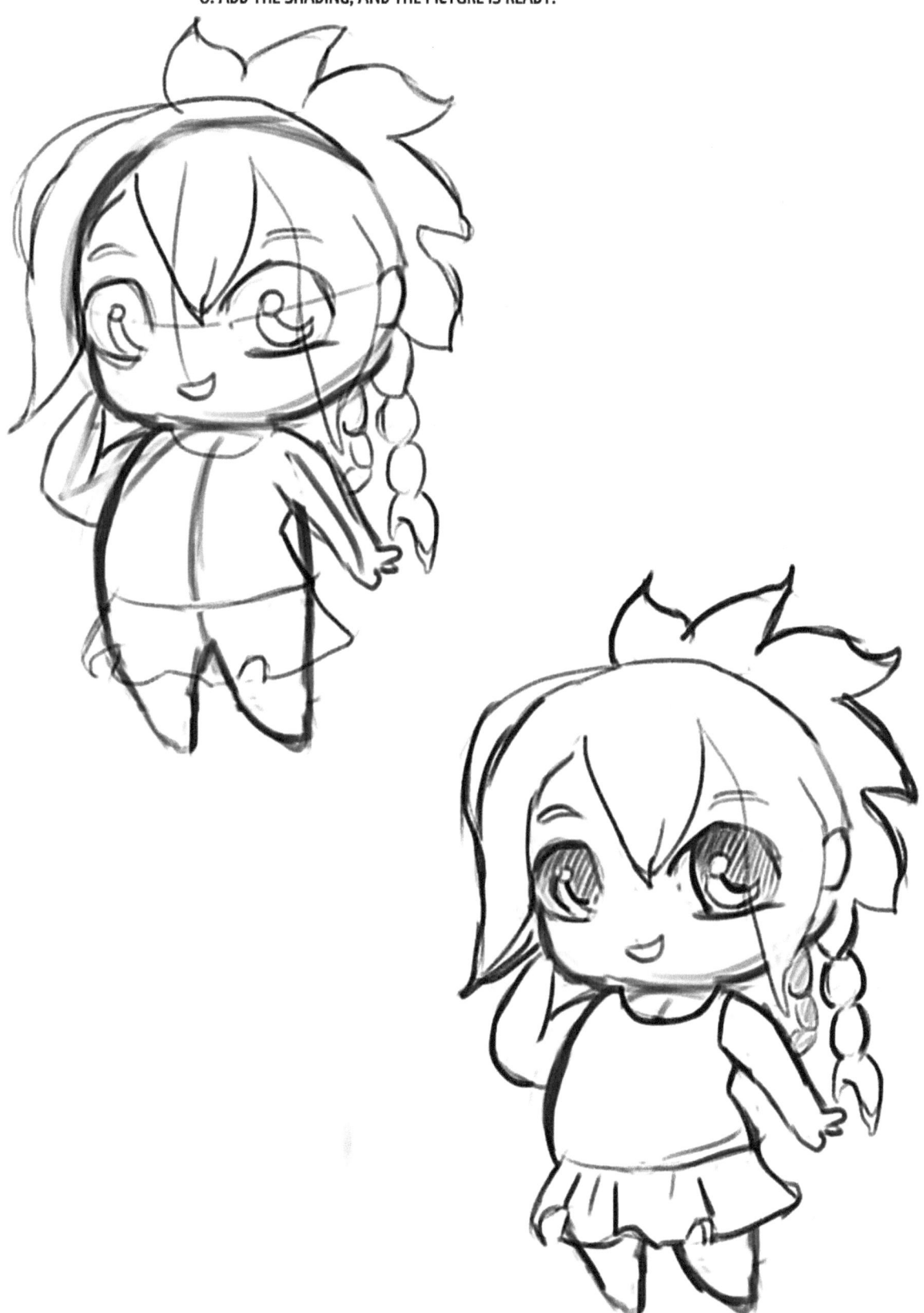

1. DRAW A FACE. MAKE THE EYES AS SHOWN
2. DRAW A BODY

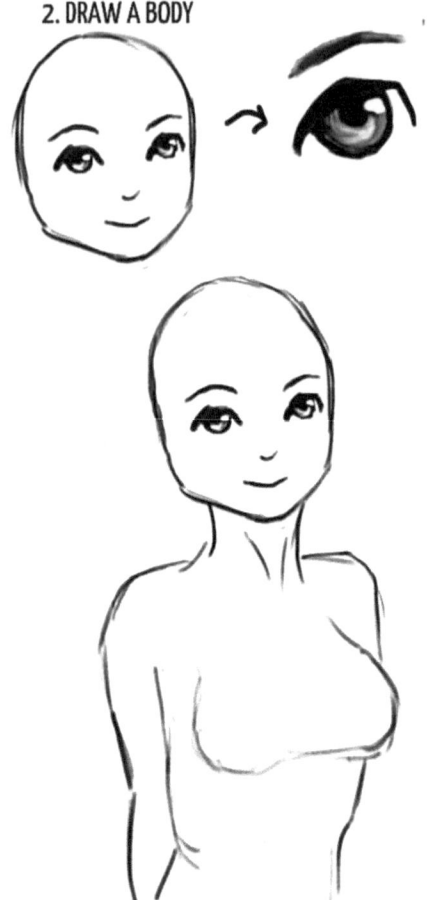

3. DRAW A HAIRSTYLE: CURLS, LOCKS, AND BANGS. ADD DETAILS TO THE CHARACTER'S COSTUME.

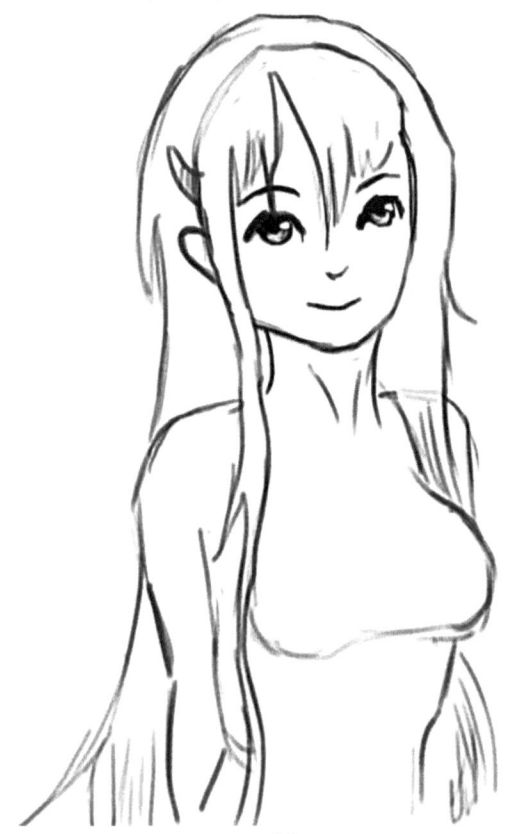

4. DRAW CHIAROSCURO ON HAIR AND CLOTHES.

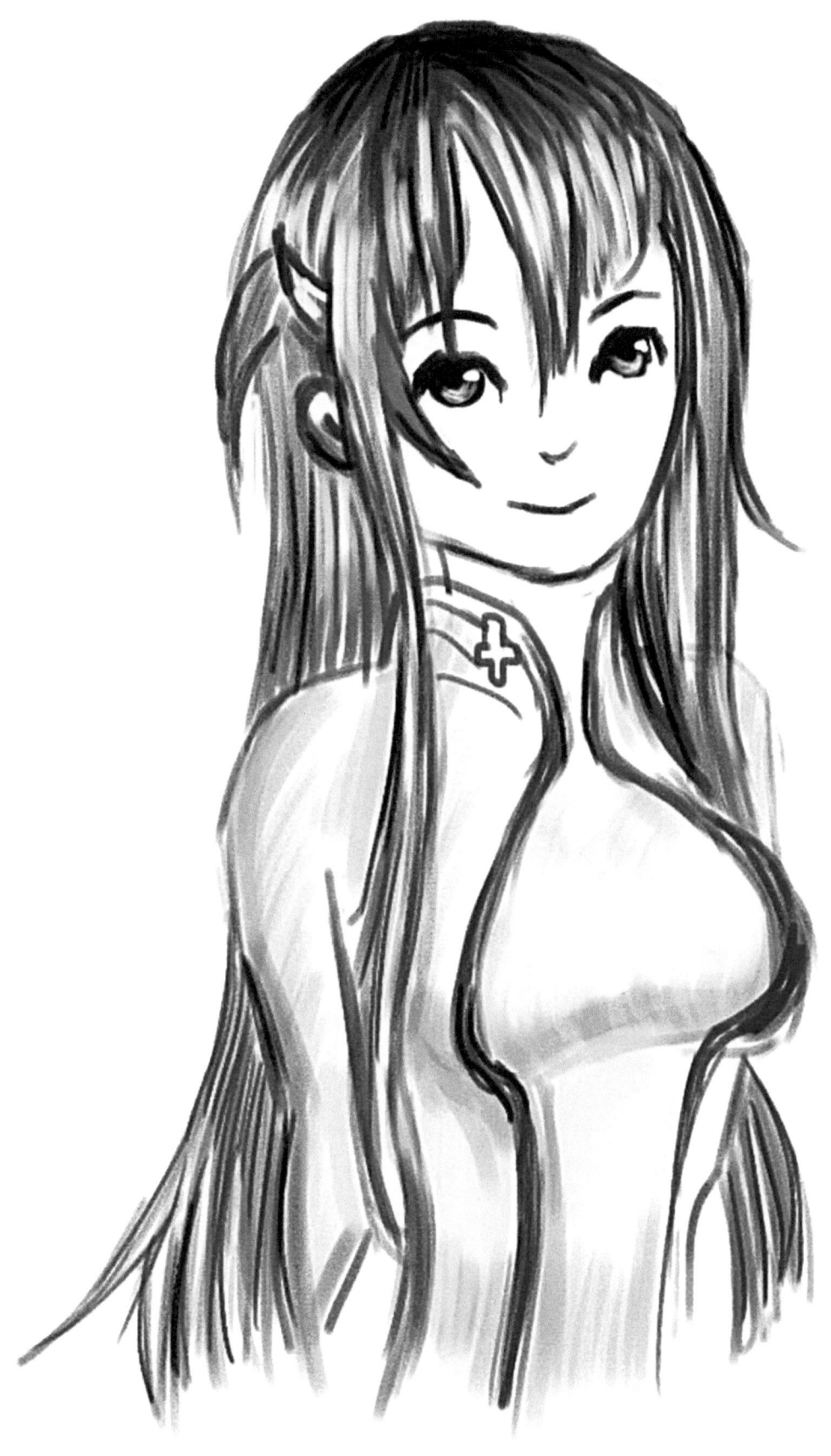

1. DRAW AN OVAL. OUTLINE THE EYES AND EYEBROWS. DRAW A NOSE AND A MOUTH.

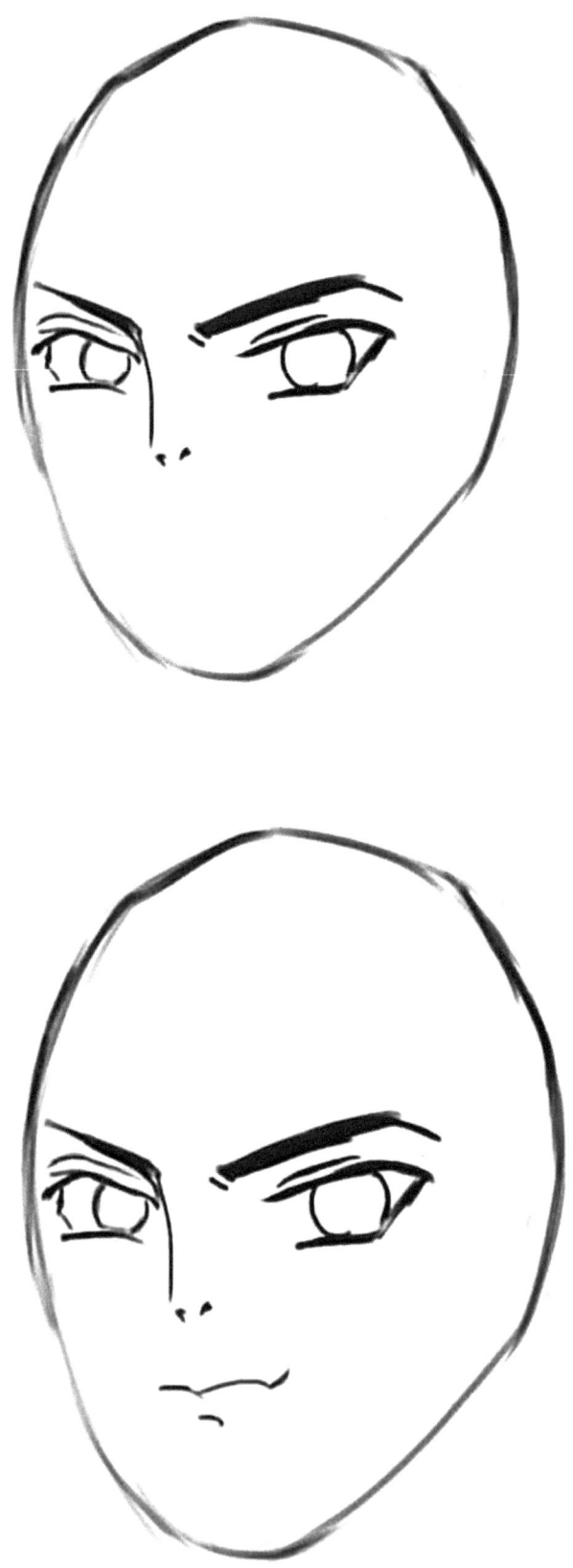

2. IMPROVING THE SHAPE OF THE FACE, FINISH THE EAR AND NECK. THE NECK SHOULD BE WIDE TO EMPHASIZE THE MASCULINITY OF THE CHARACTER.

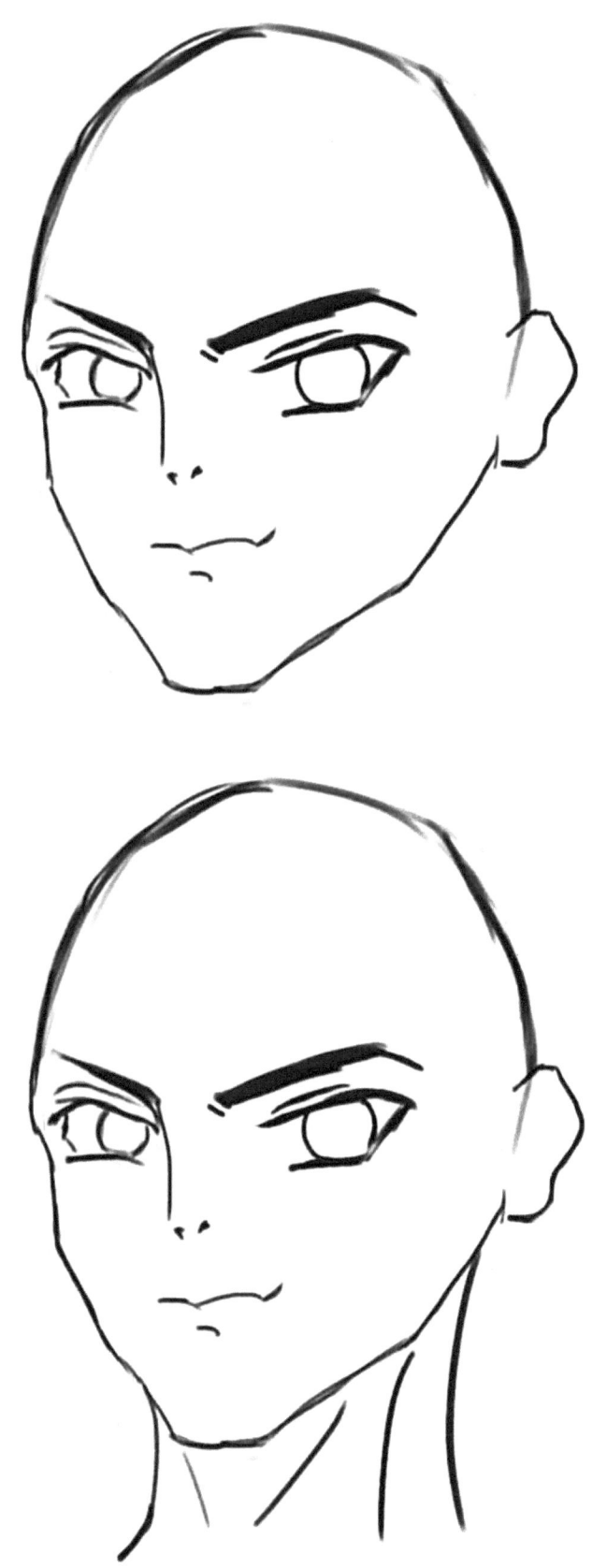

3. DRAW A SHEEN OF THE EYES IN DETAIL AS SHOWN IN THE FIGURE. ADD STRANDS OF HAIR.

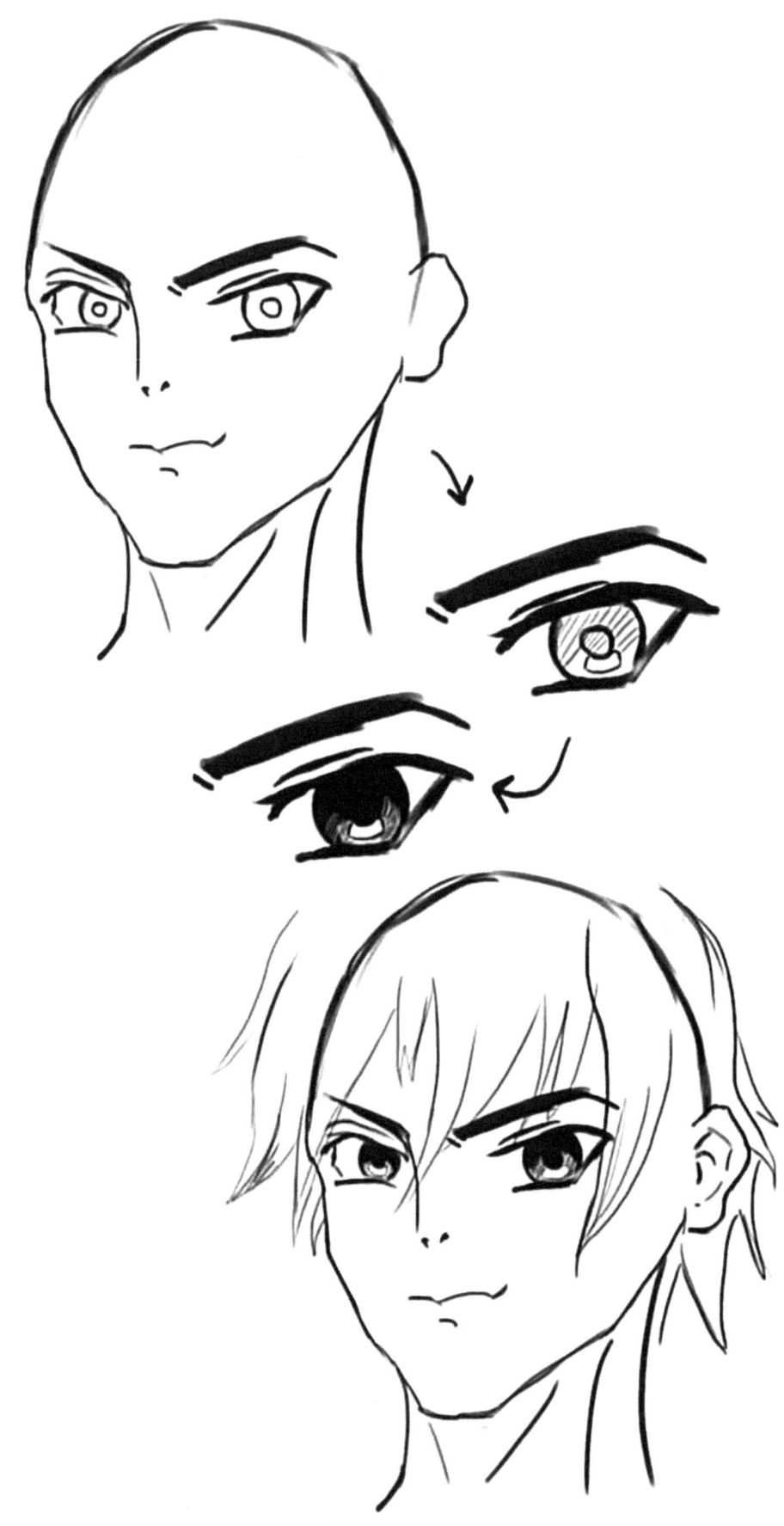

4. DRAW A SHADOW ON THE NECK FALLING ON THE CHIN. ERASE EXCESS LINES.

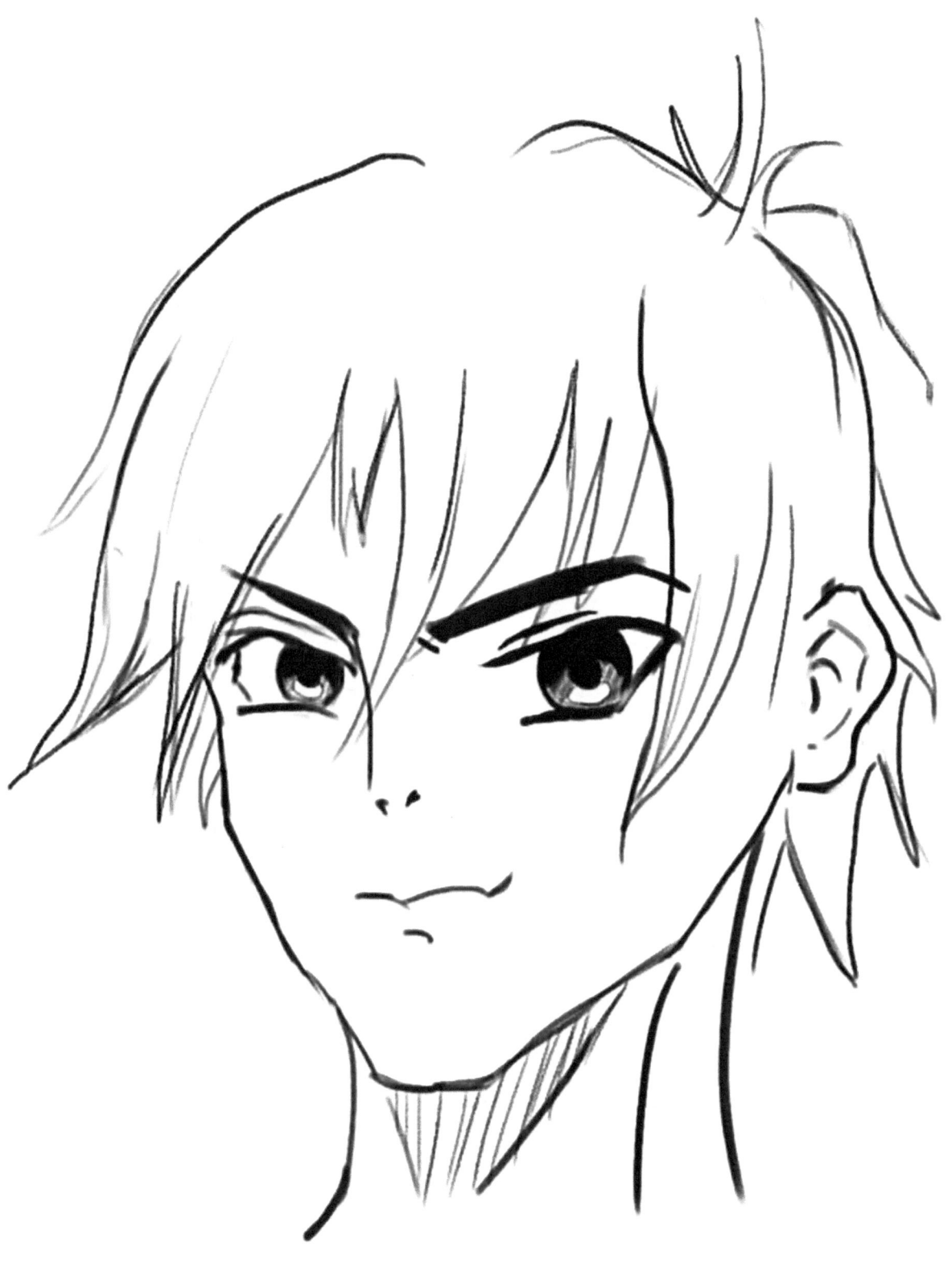

1. DRAW A BALL. INSIDE IT, DRAW TWO CIRCLES. THEY WILL BE THE CAT'S EYES.
2. GIVE THE CAT FACIAL FEATURES: EARS, NOSE, AND A MOUTH. DRAW THE EYES IN DETAIL.

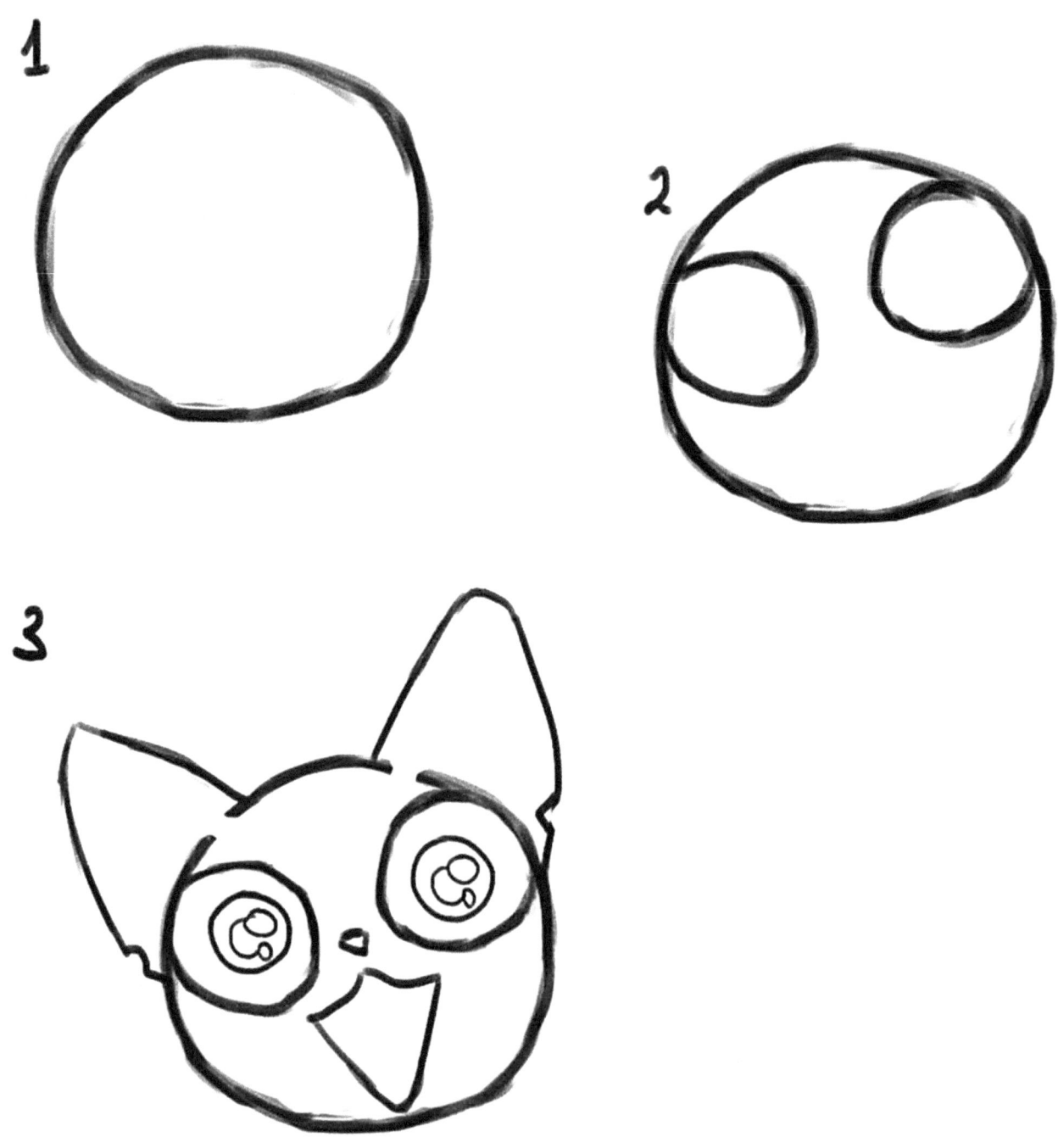

3. DRAW A TRUNK, LEGS, AND TAIL.
4. THE FINISHING TOUCHES WILL BE WHISKERS AND FUR IN THE EARS.

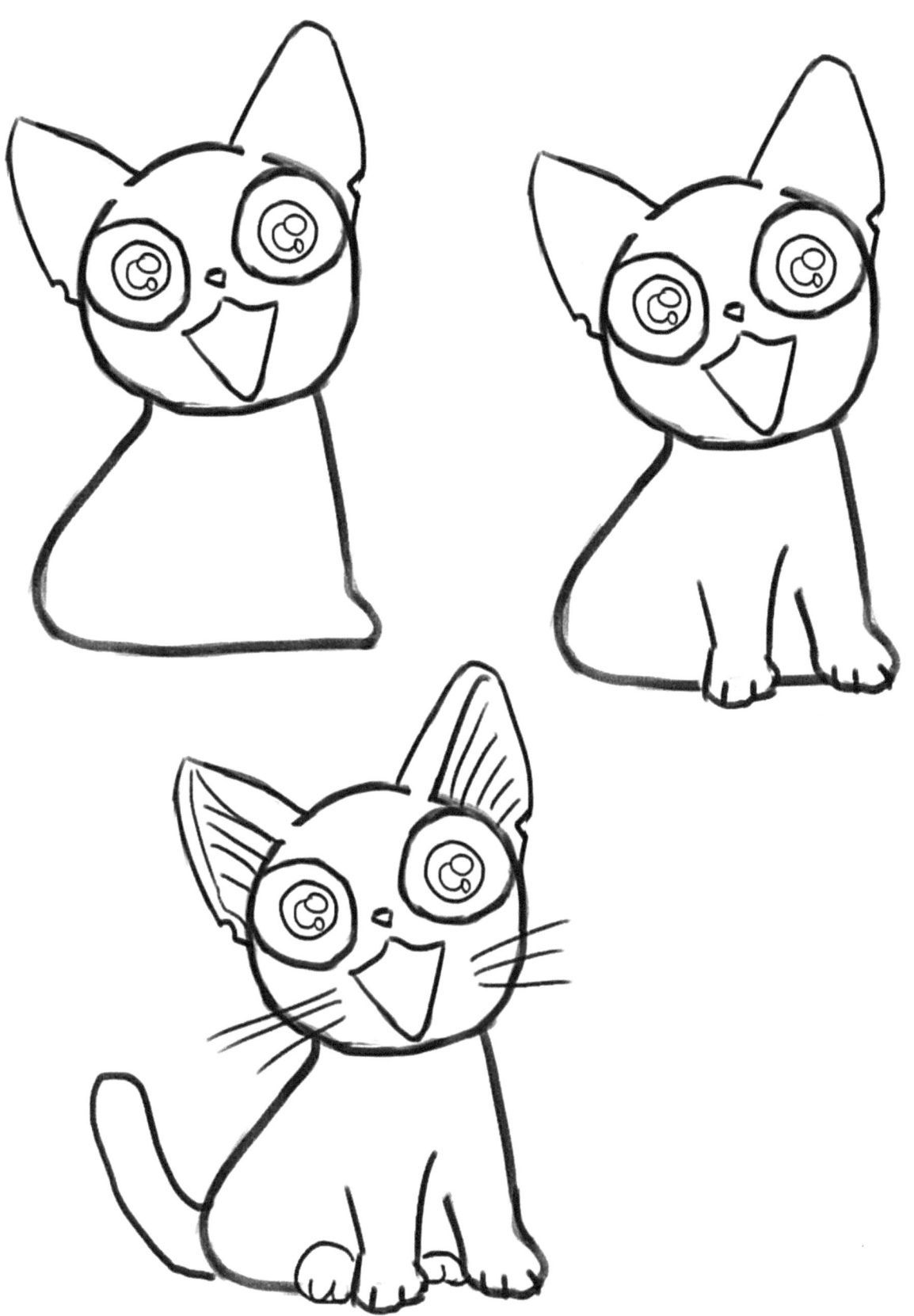

1. DRAW AN OVAL AND ADD A CHIN TO IT. DIVIDE THE RESULTING SHAPE IN HALF.
2. DRAW A STRIP IN THE SHAPE OF THE HEAD WHERE THE EYES WILL BE OUTLINED AND DRAW THEM. DRAW THE NOSE AND MOUTH.
3. DRAW HAIR, NECK, AND SHOULDERS.

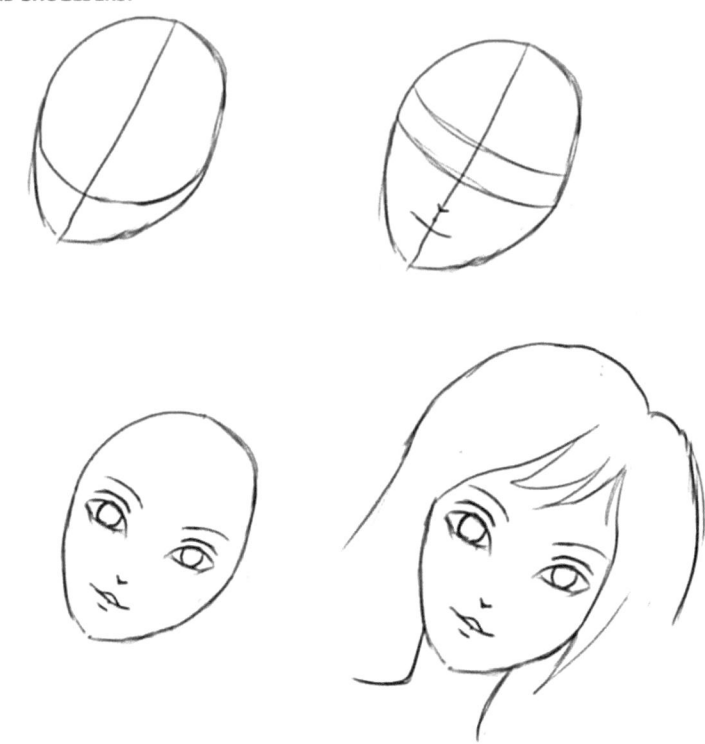

4. ELABORATE THE EYES AND COMPLEMENT THE LOCKS OF HAIR.

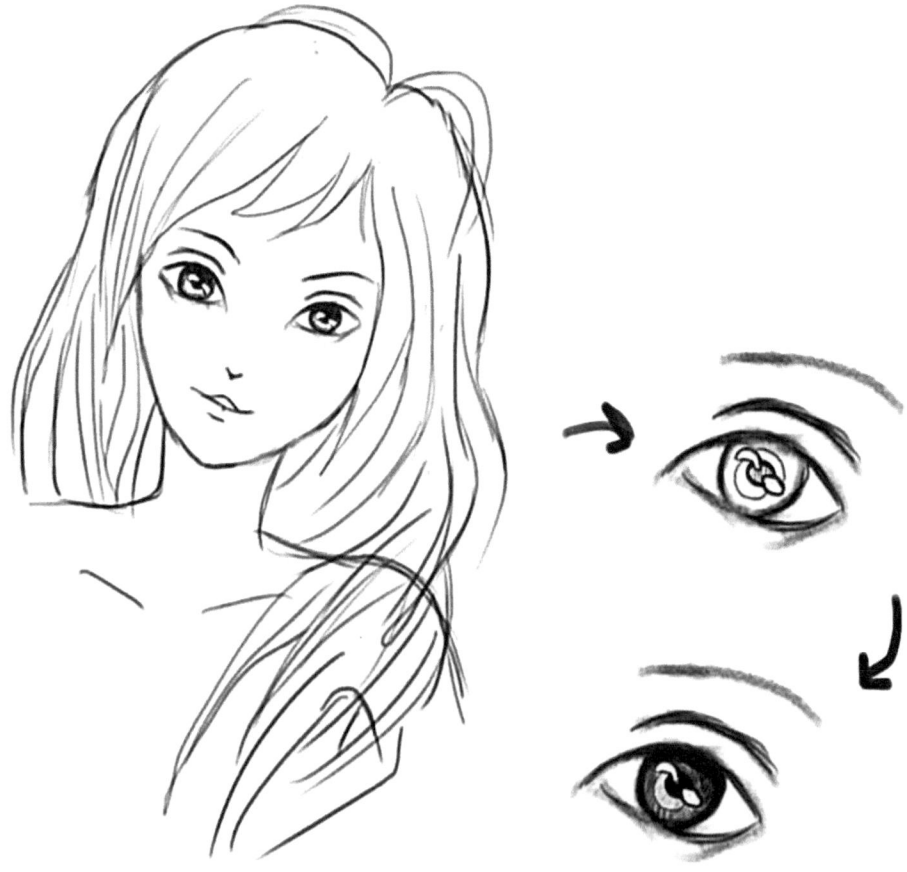

5. ON THE HAIR, DRAW SHADING. DRAW SMALL HAIRS AND STRANDS.

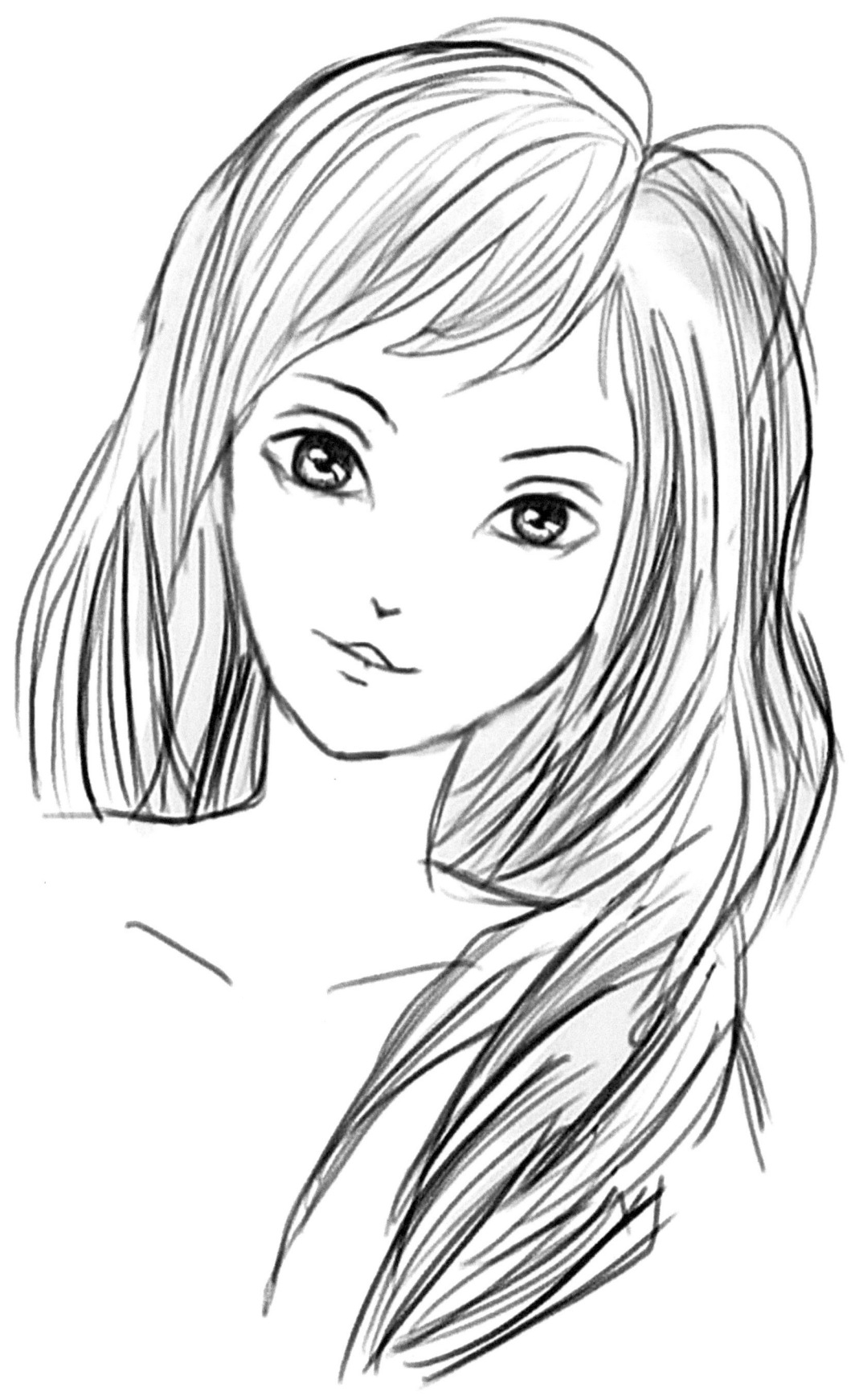

www.ingramcontent.com/pod-product-compliance
Lightning Source LLC
Chambersburg PA
CBHW040436220526
45473CB00004B/1454